Naturalization Application (for a Foreign National who has been a Legal Permanent Resident for 5 years)

Becoming a U.S. Citizen through Naturalization

Attorney Brian D. Lerner

LAW OFFICES OF
BRIAN D. LERNER
A PROFESSIONAL CORPORATION

ATTORNEY DRAFTED IMMIGRATION PETITIONS

By

Brian D. Lerner

Attorney at Law

Disclaimer and Terms of Use:

INTRODUCTION

There are a multitude of different immigration petitions and applications. They are complex and full of requirements. Obviously, it would be best to hire an immigration attorney to best prepare the petitions and applications. However, this can certainly cost thousands of dollars.

The next best option is to get a sample of the petition written by an experienced immigration attorney. The samples cost a fraction what would be charged by an immigration attorney. However, while the reader has to alter, amend and change the parts of the sample petition to reflect their actual situation, it is a fantastic roadmap for them to use. If the reader has purchased the entire petition or application, they will have real live samples of cover letters, forms, declarations, affidavits and the necessary exhibits to use. The samples come from real cases and the names of those clients have been redacted to protect the privacy of that person or corporation.

These are petitions and applications that have been drafted by an experienced immigration attorney with over 25 years of experience. Get the benefits of that experience without the costs.

CONTENTS

ATTORNEY DRAFTED IMMIGRATION PETITIONS   ii

INTRODUCTION   iii

About the Law Offices of Brian D. Lerner   v

About Naturalization Application for a Lawful Permanent Resident who has been a LPR for 5 years   vi

ATTORNEY COVER LETTER   1

FORMS   4

EXHIBITS   30

EXHIBIT '1': Applicant's Permanent Resident Card   31

EXHIBIT '2': Applicant's Divorce Decree   34

EXHIBIT '3': Applicant's Marriage Certificate   48

EXHIBIT '4': Applicant's Childrens Birth Certificate   50

EXHIBIT '5': Superior Court of California, Los Angeles County Docket Sheet (8DY07564)   57

EXHIBIT '6': Applicant's 2018 Federal Income Tax Return   65

ABOUT THE AUTHOR   85

About the Law Offices of Brian D. Lerner

The Law Offices of Brian D. Lerner, APC. The law practice consists of Immigration and Nationality Law and everything involved with and regarding immigration which includes citizenhsip, investment visas, family and employment visas, removal and deportation hearings, appeals, waivers, adjustment, consulate processing and all types of immigration and citizenship matters. Thousands of families have been reunited and/or permitted to stay in the U.S. and/or return to the U.S. because of the successful work of Immigration Attorney Brian D. Lerner.

This law offices handles all types of immigration cases including family based and employment based. Immigration issues range from immigration court proceedings to trying to fix what paralegals may have done that was neither correct nor proper. Foreign nationals must have experience lawyers admitted to practice law.

The Law Offices of Brian D. Lerner, APC, handles cases arising from business visas, work permits, Green Cards, non-immigrant visas, deportation, citizenship, appeals and all areas of immigration. The Law Offices of Brian D. Lerner, APC does EB-5 Investor Visas, H-1B Specialty Occupation, L-1 Intracompany Transferee, E-2 Treaty Investor, E-1 Treaty Trader, O-1 Extraordinary Ability among others. Regarding immigrant visas for the Green Card, the firm does PERM and advanced degree PERM, Family Petitions, and Extraordinary Alien Petitions. In addition to affirmative petitions, the Law Firm represents people in people in deportation and removal hearings, including political asylum, withholding of removal, and convention against torture cases.

Brian D. Lerner has been certified as an expert in Immigration & Nationality Law by the California State Bar, Board of Legal Specialization since 2000 and has been re-certified three times. He now passes on his decades of experience by allowing the Reader, Law Schools, Professors and other Immigration Attorneys to purchase sample petitions on every facet of Immigration   Law.

About Naturalization Application for a Lawful Permanent Resident who has been a LPR for 5 years

Naturalization is the legal process through which a foreign citizen or national can become a United States Citizen. In order to be naturalized, an applicant must first meet certain criteria to apply for citizenship. Then, the applicant must complete an application, attend an interview and pass an English and Civics test.

ATTORNEY COVER LETTER

Law Offices of Brian D. Lerner

A PROFESSIONAL CORPORATION

CERTIFIED SPECIALIST IN IMMIGRATION AND NATIONALITY LAW
ADMITTED TO THE U.S. SUPREME COURT

LONG BEACH, CALIFORNIA
(562) 495-0554

September 14, 2020

U.S. Citizenship and Immigration Services
Attn: N-400
1820 E. Skyharbor Circle S, Suite 100
Phoenix, AZ 85034

> **Re:** **N-400, Application for Naturalization**
> **Applicant:** ████████████████
> **Alien Number:** ████████████

Dear Officer:

We hereby enclose the following in support of Applicant's N-400, Application for Naturalization:

Form:	Description:
G-28	Notice of Entry of Appearance as Attorney or Accredited Representative; and
N-400	Application for Naturalization and $725.00 Filing Fee.

Table of Exhibits

Exhibit:	Description:
1.	Applicant's Permanent Resident Card;
2.	Applicant's Divorce Decree;
3.	Applicant's Marriage Certificate;
4.	Applicant's Children's Birth Certificates;
5.	Superior Court of California, Los Angeles County Docket Sheet (8DY07564); and
6.	Applicant's 2018 Federal Income Tax Return.

In the present case, Applicant is statutorily eligible for naturalization because she is at least 18-years-old, she has been a lawful permanent resident for at least five years, she has been physically present in the United States and resided in Los Angeles County, California for the requisite period prior to the filing of his application and she has been a person of good moral character throughout the statutory period. *See* INA § 310 *et seq.*; 8 C.F.R. § 316.

//
//
//

Based on the foregoing, we respectfully request that the instant application be approved.

If you should have any questions, please feel free to contact our office at (562) 495-0554.

Sincerely,

Christopher A. Reed
Attorney at Law

FORMS

Notice of Entry of Appearance
as Attorney or Accredited Representative

Department of Homeland Security

DHS
Form G-28
OMB No. 1615-0105
Expires 05/31/2021

Part 1. Information About Attorney or Accredited Representative

1. USCIS Online Account Number (if any)

   ▶ [   ]

Name of Attorney or Accredited Representative

2.a. Family Name (Last Name) **Reed**

2.b. Given Name (First Name) **Christopher**

2.c. Middle Name **Allan**

Address of Attorney or Accredited Representative

3.a. Street Number and Name **3233 E. Broadway**

3.b. ☐ Apt. ☐ Ste. ☐ Flr. [   ]

3.c. City or Town **Long Beach**

3.d. State **CA** 3.e. ZIP Code **90803**

3.f. Province [   ]

3.g. Postal Code [   ]

3.h. Country

   USA

Contact Information of Attorney or Accredited Representative

4. Daytime Telephone Number

   (562) 495-0554

5. Mobile Telephone Number (if any)

   [   ]

6. Email Address (if any)

   creed@eimmigration.org

7. Fax Number (if any)

   (562) 608-8672

Part 2. Eligibility Information for Attorney or Accredited Representative

Select all **applicable** items.

1.a. ☒ I am an attorney eligible to practice law in, and a member in good standing of, the bar of the highest courts of the following states, possessions, territories, commonwealths, or the District of Columbia. If you need extra space to complete this section, use the space provided in **Part 6. Additional Information.**

   Licensing Authority

   California Supreme Court

1.b. Bar Number (if applicable)

   235438

1.c. I (select only one box) ☒ am not ☐ am subject to any order suspending, enjoining, restraining, disbarring, or otherwise restricting me in the practice of law. If you are subject to any orders, use the space provided in **Part 6. Additional Information** to provide an explanation.

1.d. Name of Law Firm or Organization (if applicable)

   Law Offices of Brian D. Lerner, APC

2.a. ☐ I am an accredited representative of the following qualified nonprofit religious, charitable, social service, or similar organization established in the United States and recognized by the Department of Justice in accordance with 8 CFR part 1292.

2.b. Name of Recognized Organization

   [   ]

2.c. Date of Accreditation (mm/dd/yyyy)

   [   ]

3. ☐ I am associated with

   [   ]

   the attorney or accredited representative of record who previously filed Form G-28 in this case, and my appearance as an attorney or accredited representative for a limited purpose is at his or her request.

4.a. ☐ I am a law student or law graduate working under the direct supervision of the attorney or accredited representative of record on this form in accordance with the requirements in 8 CFR 292.1(a)(2).

4.b. Name of Law Student or Law Graduate

   [   ]

4867

Part 3. Notice of Appearance as Attorney or Accredited Representative

If you need extra space to complete this section, use the space provided in **Part 6. Additional Information.**

This appearance relates to immigration matters before (select **only one** box):

1.a. ☒ U.S. Citizenship and Immigration Services (USCIS)

1.b. List the form numbers or specific matter in which appearance is entered.

> N-400

2.a. ☐ U.S. Immigration and Customs Enforcement (ICE)

2.b. List the specific matter in which appearance is entered.

3.a. ☐ U.S. Customs and Border Protection (CBP)

3.b. List the specific matter in which appearance is entered.

4. Receipt Number (if any)

> ▶

5. I enter my appearance as an attorney or accredited representative at the request of the (select **only one** box):

☐ Applicant   ☒ Petitioner   ☐ Requestor
☐ Beneficiary/Derivative   ☐ Respondent (ICE, CBP)

Information About Client (Applicant, Petitioner, Requestor, Beneficiary or Derivative, Respondent, or Authorized Signatory for an Entity)

6.a. Family Name (Last Name) ▮▮▮▮▮▮▮

6.b. Given Name (First Name) ▮▮▮▮

6.c. Middle Name ▮▮▮▮

7.a. Name of Entity (if applicable)

7.b. Title of Authorized Signatory for Entity (if applicable)

8. Client's USCIS Online Account Number (if any)

> ▶

9. Client's Alien Registration Number (A-Number) (if any)

> ▶ A- ▮▮▮▮▮▮

Client's Contact Information

10. Daytime Telephone Number

> ▮▮▮▮▮▮

11. Mobile Telephone Number (if any)

> ▮▮▮▮▮▮

12. Email Address (if any)

> ▮▮▮▮▮▮

Mailing Address of Client

NOTE: Provide the client's mailing address. **Do not** provide the business mailing address of the attorney or accredited representative **unless** it serves as the safe mailing address on the application or petition being filed with this Form G-28.

13.a. Street Number and Name ▮▮▮▮▮▮

13.b. ☐ Apt. ☐ Ste. ☐ Flr.

13.c. City or Town Wilmington

13.d. State CA   13.e. ZIP Code 90744

13.f. Province

13.g. Postal Code

13.h. Country

> USA

Part 4. Client's Consent to Representation and Signature

Consent to Representation and Release of Information

I have requested the representation of and consented to being represented by the attorney or accredited representative named in **Part 1.** of this form. According to the Privacy Act of 1974 and U.S. Department of Homeland Security (DHS) policy, I also consent to the disclosure to the named attorney or accredited representative of any records pertaining to me that appear in any system of records of USCIS, ICE, or CBP.

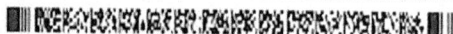

Part 4. Client's Consent to Representation and Signature (continued)

Options Regarding Receipt of USCIS Notices and Documents

USCIS will send notices to both a represented party (the client) and his, her, or its attorney or accredited representative either through mail or electronic delivery. USCIS will send all secure identity documents and Travel Documents to the client's U.S. mailing address.

If you want to have notices and/or secure identity documents sent to your attorney or accredited representative of record rather than to you, please select all applicable items below. You may change these elections through written notice to USCIS.

1.a. [X] I request that USCIS send original notices on an application or petition to the business address of my attorney or accredited representative as listed in this form.

1.b. [ ] I request that USCIS send any secure identity document (Permanent Resident Card, Employment Authorization Document, or Travel Document) that I receive to the U.S. business address of my attorney or accredited representative (or to a designated military or diplomatic address in a foreign country (if permitted)).

NOTE: If your notice contains Form I-94, Arrival-Departure Record, USCIS will send the notice to the U.S. business address of your attorney or accredited representative. If you would rather have your Form I-94 sent directly to you, select Item Number 1.c.

1.c. [ ] I request that USCIS send my notice containing Form I-94 to me at my U.S. mailing address.

Signature of Client or Authorized Signatory for an Entity

2.a. Signature of Client or Authorized Signatory for an Entity

⇨

2.b. Date of Signature (mm/dd/yyyy)   09/11/2020

Part 5. Signature of Attorney or Accredited Representative

I have read and understand the regulations and conditions contained in 8 CFR 103.2 and 292 governing appearances and representation before DHS. I declare under penalty of perjury under the laws of the United States that the information I have provided on this form is true and correct.

1.a. Signature of Attorney or Accredited Representative

1.b. Date of Signature (mm/dd/yyyy)   09/11/2020

2.a. Signature of Law Student or Law Graduate

2.b. Date of Signature (mm/dd/yyyy)

Part 6. Additional Information

If you need extra space to provide any additional information within this form, use the space below. If you need more space than what is provided, you may make copies of this page to complete and file with this form or attach a separate sheet of paper. Type or print your name at the top of each sheet; indicate the **Page Number, Part Number,** and **Item Number** to which your answer refers; and sign and date each sheet.

1.a Family Name
(Last Name) ████████████████

1.b. Given Name
(First Name) ██████

1.c. Middle Name ██████████

2.a. Page Number   **2.b.** Part Number   **2.c.** Item Number

2.d.

3.a. Page Number   **3.b.** Part Number   **3.c.** Item Number

3.d.

4.a. Page Number   **4.b.** Part Number   **4.c.** Item Number

4.d.

5.a. Page Number   **5.b.** Part Number   **5.c.** Item Number

5.d.

6.a. Page Number   **6.b.** Part Number   **6.c.** Item Number

6.d.

Application for Naturalization

Department of Homeland Security
U.S. Citizenship and Immigration Services

USCIS
Form N-400
OMB No. 1615-0052
Expires 09/30/2022

For USCIS Use Only	Date Stamp	Receipt	Action Block
Remarks			

▶ **START HERE - Type or print in black ink.** Type or print "N/A" if an item is not applicable or the answer is none, unless otherwise indicated. Failure to answer all of the questions may delay U.S. Citizenship and Immigration Services (USCIS) processing your Form N-400. **NOTE: You must complete Parts 1. - 15.**

If your biological or legal adoptive mother or father is a U.S. citizen by birth, or was naturalized before you reached your 18th birthday, you may already be a U.S. citizen. Before you consider filing this application, please visit the USCIS Website at www.uscis.gov for more information on this topic and to review the instructions for Form N-600, Application for Certificate of Citizenship, and Form N-600K, Application for Citizenship and Issuance of Certificate Under Section 322.

NOTE: Are either of your parents a United States citizen? If you answer "Yes," then complete **Part 6. Information About Your Parents** as part of this application. If you answer "No," then skip **Part 6.** and go to **Part 7. Biographic Information.**

Part 1. Information About Your Eligibility (Select only one box or your Form N-400 may be delayed)

Enter Your 9 Digit A-Number:
▶ A- �_____

1. You are at least 18 years of age **and:**

   A. ☒ Have been a lawful permanent resident of the United States for at least 5 years.

   B. ☐ Have been a lawful permanent resident of the United States for at least 3 years. In addition, you have been married to and living with the same U.S. citizen spouse for the last 3 years, **and** your spouse has been a U.S. citizen for the last 3 years at the time you filed your Form N-400.

   C. ☐ Are a lawful permanent resident of the United States **and** you are the spouse of a U.S. citizen **and** your U.S. citizen spouse is regularly engaged in specified employment abroad. (See the Immigration and Nationality Act (INA) section 319(b).) If your residential address is outside the United States and you are filing under Section 319(b), select the USCIS Field Office from the list below where you would like to have your naturalization interview:

   _____

   D. ☐ Are applying on the basis of qualifying military service.

   E. ☐ Other (Explain): _____

Part 2. Information About You (Person applying for naturalization)

1. Your Current Legal Name (**do not provide a nickname**)

Family Name (Last Name)	Given Name (First Name)	Middle Name (if applicable)
▮▮▮▮▮▮▮▮	▮▮▮▮	Alejandra

2. Your Name Exactly As It Appears on Your Permanent Resident Card (if applicable)

Family Name (Last Name)	Given Name (First Name)	Middle Name (if applicable)
▮▮▮▮▮▮▮▮	▮▮▮▮	A

3. Other Names You Have Used Since Birth (include nicknames, aliases, and maiden name, if applicable)

Family Name (Last Name)	Given Name (First Name)	Middle Name (if applicable)
██████████	███	Alejandra

4. Name Change (Optional)

   Read the Form N-400 Instructions before you decide whether or not you would like to legally change your name.

   Would you like to legally change your name?   ☐ Yes ☒ No

   If you answered "Yes," type or print the new name you would like to use in the spaces provided below.

Family Name (Last Name)	Given Name (First Name)	Middle Name (if applicable)

5. U.S. Social Security Number (if applicable)   6. USCIS Online Account Number (if any)

   ▶ [████████]   ▶ [   ]

7. Gender   8. Date of Birth   9. Date You Became a Lawful
   ☐ Male ☒ Female   (mm/dd/yyyy)   Permanent Resident (mm/dd/yyyy)
                      07/21/1980   04/25/2003

10. Country of Birth   11. Country of Citizenship or Nationality

    Mexico   Mexico

12. Do you have a physical or developmental disability or mental impairment that prevents you from   ☐ Yes ☒ No
    demonstrating your knowledge and understanding of the English language and/or civics requirements
    for naturalization?

    If you answered "Yes," submit a completed Form N-648, Medical Certification for Disability Exceptions, when you file your
    Form N-400.

13. Exemptions from the English Language Test

    A. Are you **50 years of age or older** and have you lived in the United States as a lawful permanent   ☐ Yes ☒ No
       resident for periods totaling at least **20 years** at the time you file your Form N-400?

    B. Are you **55 years of age or older** and have you lived in the United States as a lawful permanent   ☐ Yes ☒ No
       resident for periods totaling at least **15 years** at the time you file your Form N-400?

    C. Are you **65 years of age or older** and have you lived in the United States as a lawful permanent   ☐ Yes ☒ No
       resident for periods totaling at least **20 years** at the time you file your Form N-400? (If you meet
       this requirement, you will also be given a simplified version of the civics test.)

Part 3. Accommodations for Individuals With Disabilities and/or Impairments

NOTE: Read the information in the Form N-400 Instructions before completing this part.

1. Are you requesting an accommodation because of your disabilities and/or impairments?   ☐ Yes ☒ No

   If you answered "Yes," select any applicable box.

   A. ☐ I am deaf or hard of hearing and request the following accommodation. (If you are requesting a sign-language
         interpreter, indicate for which language (for example, American Sign Language).)

         [   ]

   B. ☐ I am blind or have low vision and request the following accommodation:

         [   ]

Part 3. Accommodations for Individuals With Disabilities and/or Impairments (continued)

A- ████████

    C.   ☐ I have another type of disability and/or impairment (for example, use a wheelchair). (Describe the nature of your disability and/or impairment and the accommodation you are requesting.)

                      [   ]

Part 4. Information to Contact You

1. Daytime Telephone Number
    ████████████

2. Work Telephone Number (if any)
    ████████████

3. Evening Telephone Number
    ████████████

4. Mobile Telephone Number (if any)
    ████████████

5. Email Address (if any)
    ████████████

Part 5. Information About Your Residence

1. Where have you lived during the last five years? Provide your most recent residence and then list every location where you have lived during the last five years. If you need extra space, use additional sheets of paper.

    A. Current Physical Address

Street Number and Name	Apt.	Ste.	Flr.	Number
████████████	☐	☐	☐

City or Town	County	State	ZIP Code + 4
Wilmington	Los Angeles	CA	90744 -

Province or Region (foreign address only)	Postal Code (foreign address only)	Country (foreign address only)
		USA

Dates of Residence	From (mm/dd/yyyy)	To (mm/dd/yyyy)
	03/2018	Present

    B. Current Mailing Address (if different from the address above)

In Care Of Name (if any)
N/A

Street Number and Name	Apt.	Ste.	Flr.	Number
N/A	☐	☐	☐	N/A

City or Town	County	State	ZIP Code + 4
N/A	N/A	N/A	N/A - N/A

Province or Region (foreign address only)	Postal Code (foreign address only)	Country (foreign address only)
N/A	N/A	N/A

A-███████████

C. Physical Address 2

Street Number and Name

███████████

Apt. ☐ Ste. ☐ Flr. ☐ Number [ ]

City or Town	County	State	ZIP Code + 4
Long Beach	Los Angeles	CA	90804 - [ ]

Province or Region (foreign address only)	Postal Code (foreign address only)	Country (foreign address only)
[ ]	[ ]	USA

Dates of Residence

From (mm/dd/yyyy): 11/01/2013

To (mm/dd/yyyy): 03/2018

D. Physical Address 3

Street Number and Name

N/A

Apt. ☐ Ste. ☐ Flr. ☐ Number N/A

City or Town	County	State	ZIP Code + 4
N/A	N/A	N/A	N/A - N/A

Province or Region (foreign address only)	Postal Code (foreign address only)	Country (foreign address only)
N/A	N/A	N/A

Dates of Residence

From (mm/dd/yyyy): N/A

To (mm/dd/yyyy): N/A

E. Physical Address 4

Street Number and Name

N/A

Apt. ☐ Ste. ☐ Flr. ☐ Number N/A

City or Town	County	State	ZIP Code + 4
N/A	N/A	N/A	N/A - N/A

Province or Region (foreign address only)	Postal Code (foreign address only)	Country (foreign address only)
N/A	N/A	N/A

Dates of Residence

From (mm/dd/yyyy): N/A

To (mm/dd/yyyy): N/A

Part 6. Information About Your Parents

If neither one of your parents is a United States citizen, then skip this part and go to Part 7.

1. Were your parents married before your 18th birthday? ☐ Yes ☒ No

Information About Your Mother

2. Is your mother a U.S. citizen? ☐ Yes ☒ No

   If you answered "Yes," complete the following information. If you answered "No," go to **Item Number 3.**

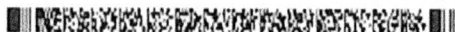

Part 6. Information About Your Parents (continued)

A- ▓▓▓▓▓▓▓▓▓▓

A. Current Legal Name of U.S. Citizen Mother

Family Name (Last Name)	Given Name (First Name)	Middle Name (if applicable)

B. Mother's Country of Birth

C. Mother's Date of Birth (mm/dd/yyyy)

D. Date Mother Became a U.S. Citizen (if known) (mm/dd/yyyy)

E. Mother's A-Number (if any)

▶ A-

Information About Your Father

3. Is your father a U.S. citizen? ☐ Yes ☒ No

If you answered "Yes," complete the information below. If you answered "No," go to **Part 7.**

A. Current Legal Name of U.S. Citizen Father

Family Name (Last Name)	Given Name (First Name)	Middle Name (if applicable)

B. Father's Country of Birth

C. Father's Date of Birth (mm/dd/yyyy)

D. Date Father Became a U.S. Citizen (if known) (mm/dd/yyyy)

E. Father's A-Number (if any)

▶ A-

Part 7. Biographic Information

NOTE: USCIS requires you to complete the categories below to conduct background checks. (See the Form N-400 Instructions for more information.)

1. Ethnicity (Select **only one** box)

   ☒ Hispanic or Latino ☐ Not Hispanic or Latino

2. Race (Select **all applicable** boxes)

   ☒ White ☐ Asian ☐ Black or African American ☐ American Indian or Alaska Native ☐ Native Hawaiian or Other Pacific Islander

3. Height Feet 5   Inches 3   4. Weight Pounds 1 4 0

5. Eye color (Select **only one** box)

   ☐ Black ☐ Blue ☒ Brown ☐ Gray ☐ Green ☐ Hazel ☐ Maroon ☐ Pink ☐ Unknown/Other

6. Hair color (Select **only one** box)

   ☐ Bald (No hair) ☐ Black ☐ Blond ☒ Brown ☐ Gray ☐ Red ☐ Sandy ☐ White ☐ Unknown/Other

Part 8. Information About Your Employment and Schools You Attended A- ███████

List where you have worked or attended school full time or part time during the last five years. Provide information for the complete time period. Include all military, police, and/or intelligence service. Begin by providing information about your most recent or current employment, studies, or unemployment (if applicable). Provide the locations and dates where you worked, were self-employed, were unemployed, or have studied for the last five years. If you worked for yourself, type or print "self-employed." If you were unemployed, type or print "unemployed." If you need extra space, use additional sheets of paper.

1. Employer or School Name

   Self-Employed: ███████

   Street Number and Name ███████ Apt. ☐ Ste. ☐ Flr. ☐ Number

City or Town	State	ZIP Code + 4
Long Beach	CA	90804 -

   Province or Region (foreign address only) | Postal Code (foreign address only) | Country (foreign address only)

Date From (mm/dd/yyyy)	Date To (mm/dd/yyyy)	Your Occupation
01/01/2012	PRESENT	Insurance

2. Employer or School Name

   N/A

   Street Number and Name N/A Apt. ☐ Ste. ☐ Flr. ☐ Number N/A

   City or Town N/A State N/A ZIP Code + 4 N/A - N/A

   Province or Region (foreign address only) N/A | Postal Code (foreign address only) N/A | Country (foreign address only) N/A

   Date From (mm/dd/yyyy) N/A | Date To (mm/dd/yyyy) N/A | Your Occupation N/A

3. Employer or School Name

   N/A

   Street Number and Name N/A Apt. ☐ Ste. ☐ Flr. ☐ Number N/A

   City or Town N/A State N/A ZIP Code + 4 N/A - N/A

   Province or Region (foreign address only) N/A | Postal Code (foreign address only) N/A | Country (foreign address only) N/A

   Date From (mm/dd/yyyy) N/A | Date To (mm/dd/yyyy) N/A | Your Occupation N/A

 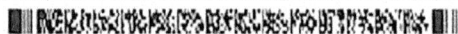

Part 9. Time Outside the United States

A- ▬▬▬▬▬▬▬▬▬

1. How many **total days (24 hours or longer)** did you spend outside the United States during the last 5 years? `0` days

2. How many trips of **24 hours or longer** have you taken outside the United States during the last 5 years? `0` trips

3. List below all the trips of **24 hours or longer** that you have taken outside the United States during the last 5 years. Start with your most recent trip and work backwards. If you need extra space, use additional sheets of paper.

Date You Left the United States (mm/dd/yyyy)	Date You Returned to the United States (mm/dd/yyyy)	Did Trip Last 6 Months or More?	Countries to Which You Traveled	Total Days Outside the United States
		☐ Yes ☐ No		
		☐ Yes ☐ No		
		☐ Yes ☐ No		
		☐ Yes ☐ No		
		☐ Yes ☐ No		
		☐ Yes ☐ No		

Part 10. Information About Your Marital History

1. What is your current marital status?

   ☐ Single, Never Married ☒ Married ☐ Divorced ☐ Widowed ☐ Separated ☐ Marriage Annulled

   If you are single and have **never** married, go to **Part 11.**

2. If you are married, is your spouse a current member of the U.S. armed forces? ☐ Yes ☒ No

3. How many times have you been married (including annulled marriages, marriages to other people, and marriages to the same person)? `2`

4. If you are married now, provide the following information about your current spouse.

   A. Current Spouse's Legal Name

Family Name (Last Name)	Given Name (First Name)	Middle Name (if applicable)
████████	████	N/A

   B. Current Spouse's Previous Legal Name

Family Name (Last Name)	Given Name (First Name)	Middle Name (if applicable)
████████	████	

   C. Other Names Used by Current Spouse (include nicknames, aliases, and maiden name, if applicable)

Family Name (Last Name)	Given Name (First Name)	Middle Name (if applicable)
N/A	N/A	N/A

   D. Current Spouse's Date of Birth (mm/dd/yyyy)   E. Date You Entered into Marriage with Current Spouse (mm/dd/yyyy)

   `12/17/1983`   `05/29/2018`

F. Current Spouse's Present Home Address

Street Number and Name   Apt. Ste. Flr. Number
▇▇▇▇▇▇▇▇▇   ☐   ☐   ☐   ☐

City or Town	County	State	ZIP Code + 4
Wilmington	Los Angeles	CA	90744 -

Province or Region   Postal Code   Country
(foreign address only)   (foreign address only)   (foreign address only)

G. Current Spouse's Current Employer or Company

N/A

5. Is your current spouse a U.S. citizen?   ☐ Yes ☒ No

If you answered "Yes," answer **Item Number 6.** If you answered "No," go to **Item Number 7.**

6. If your current spouse is a U.S. citizen, complete the following information.

A. When did your current spouse become a U.S. citizen?

☐ At Birth - Go to **Item Number 8.**   ☐ Other - Complete the following information.

B. Date Your Current Spouse Became
   a U.S. Citizen (mm/dd/yyyy)

7. If your current spouse is not a U.S. citizen, complete the following information.

A. Current Spouse's Country of Citizenship or Nationality   B. Current Spouse's A-Number (if any)

Mexico   ▶ A-

C. Current Spouse's Immigration Status
   ☐ Lawful Permanent Resident   ☒ Other (Explain): No Status

8. How many times has your current spouse been married (including annulled marriages, marriages to   [1]
   other people, and marriages to the same person)? If your current spouse has been married before,
   provide the following information about your current spouse's prior spouse.

If your current spouse has had more than one previous marriage, provide that information on additional sheets of paper.

A. Legal Name of My Current Spouse's Prior Spouse

Family Name (Last Name)	Given Name (First Name)	Middle Name (if applicable)
N/A	N/A	N/A

B. Immigration Status of My Current Spouse's Prior Spouse (if known)
   ☐ U.S. Citizen   ☐ Lawful Permanent Resident   ☐ Other (Explain):

C. Date of Birth of My Current Spouse's   D. Country of Birth of My Current Spouse's
   Prior Spouse (mm/dd/yyyy)   Prior Spouse

   N/A   N/A

E. Country of Citizenship or Nationality of My Current
   Spouse's Prior Spouse

   N/A

 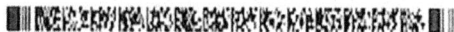

Part 10. Information About Your Marital History (continued) A-████████████

F. My Current Spouse's Date of Marriage with Prior Spouse (mm/dd/yyyy)

[N/A]

G. Date My Current Spouse's Marriage Ended with Prior Spouse (mm/dd/yyyy)

[N/A]

H. How My Current Spouse's Marriage Ended with Prior Spouse

☐ Annulled ☐ Divorced ☐ Spouse Deceased ☐ Other (Explain): [   ]

9. If you were married before, provide the following information about your prior spouse. If you have more than one previous marriage, provide that information on additional sheets of paper.

A. My Prior Spouse's Legal Name

Family Name (Last Name)	Given Name (First Name)	Middle Name (if applicable)
██████████	▪▪▪	████

B. My Prior Spouse's Immigration Status When My Marriage Ended (if known)

☒ U.S. Citizen ☐ Lawful Permanent Resident ☐ Other (Explain): [   ]

C. My Prior Spouse's Date of Birth (mm/dd/yyyy)

[04/22/1981]

D. My Prior Spouse's Country of Birth

[USA]

E. My Prior Spouse's Country of Citizenship or Nationality

[USA]

F. Date of Marriage with My Prior Spouse (mm/dd/yyyy)

[04/21/2001]

G. Date Marriage Ended with My Prior Spouse (mm/dd/yyyy)

[06/12/2012]

H. How Marriage Ended with My Prior Spouse

☐ Annulled ☒ Divorced ☐ Spouse Deceased ☐ Other (Explain): [   ]

Part 11. Information About Your Children

1. Indicate your total number of children. (You must indicate **ALL** children, including: children who are alive, missing, or deceased; children born in the United States or in other countries; children under 18 years of age or older; children who are currently married or unmarried; children living with you or elsewhere; current stepchildren; legally adopted children; **and** children born when you were not married.) [6]

2. Provide the following information about all your children (sons and daughters) listed in **Item Number 1.**, regardless of age. To list any additional children, use additional sheets of paper.

A. Child 1

Current Legal Name

Family Name (Last Name)	Given Name (First Name)	Middle Name (if applicable)
██████████	████	███

A-Number (if any) ► A- [N/A]

Date of Birth (mm/dd/yyyy) [05/15/1999]

Country of Birth [USA]

 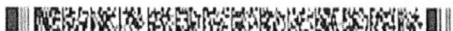

Current Address

Street Number and Name   Apt. Ste. Flr. Number

■■■■■■■■■■■   ☐   ☐   ☐

City or Town	County	State	ZIP Code + 4
Long Beach	Los Angeles	CA	90813 -

Province or Region (foreign address only)	Postal Code (foreign address only)	Country (foreign address only)
		USA

What is your child's relationship to you? (for example, biological child, stepchild, legally adopted child)   **Biological Child**

B. Child 2

Current Legal Name

Family Name (Last Name)	Given Name (First Name)	Middle Name (if applicable)
■■■■■■	■■■■■■	■■■■■■

A-Number (if any)   Date of Birth (mm/dd/yyyy) Country of Birth

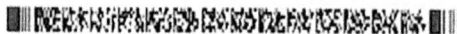

▶ A-   10/10/2000   USA

Current Address

Street Number and Name   Apt. Ste. Flr. Number

■■■■■■■■■■   ☐   ☐   ☐

City or Town	County	State	ZIP Code + 4
Wilmington	Los Angeles	CA	90744 -

Province or Region (foreign address only)	Postal Code (foreign address only)	Country (foreign address only)
		USA

What is your child's relationship to you? (for example, biological child, stepchild, legally adopted child)   **Biological Child**

C. Child 3

Current Legal Name

Family Name (Last Name)	Given Name (First Name)	Middle Name (if applicable)
CA■■■■■	■■■■■	■■■■■

A-Number (if any)   Date of Birth (mm/dd/yyyy) Country of Birth

▶ A-   01/11/2003   USA

Part 11. Information About Your Children (continued) A- ■■■■■■■■3

Current Address

Street Number and Name ■■■■■■■ | Apt. ☐ Ste. ☐ Flr. ☐ Number ☐

City or Town	County	State	ZIP Code + 4
Wilmington	Los Angeles	CA	90744 -

Province or Region (foreign address only)	Postal Code (foreign address only)	Country (foreign address only)
		USA

What is your child's relationship to you? (for example, biological child, stepchild, legally adopted child) **Biological Child**

D. Child 4

Current Legal Name

Family Name (Last Name)	Given Name (First Name)	Middle Name (if applicable)
■■■■■■	■■■■	

A-Number (if any)	Date of Birth (mm/dd/yyyy)	Country of Birth
► A-	08/17/2011	USA

Current Address

Street Number and Name ■■■■■■■■■■ | Apt. ☐ Ste. ☐ Flr. ☐ Number ☐

City or Town	County	State	ZIP Code + 4
Wilmington	Los Angeles	CA	90744 -

Province or Region (foreign address only)	Postal Code (foreign address only)	Country (foreign address only)
		USA

What is your child's relationship to you? (for example, biological child, stepchild, legally adopted child) **Biological Child**

Part 12. Additional Information About You (Person Applying for Naturalization)

Answer Item Numbers 1. - 21. If you answer "Yes" to any of these questions, include a typed or printed explanation on additional sheets of paper.

1. Have you **EVER** claimed to be a U.S. citizen (in writing or any other way)? ☐ Yes ☒ No

2. Have you **EVER** registered to vote in any Federal, state, or local election in the United States? ☐ Yes ☒ No

3. Have you **EVER** voted in any Federal, state, or local election in the United States? ☐ Yes ☒ No

4. A. Do you now have, or did you **EVER** have, a hereditary title or an order of nobility in any foreign country? ☐ Yes ☒ No

   B. If you answered "Yes," are you willing to give up any inherited titles or orders of nobility that you have in a foreign country at your naturalization ceremony? ☐ Yes ☐ No

5. Have you **EVER** been declared legally incompetent or been confined to a mental institution? ☐ Yes ☒ No

---

Form N-400 Edition 09/17/19 ▐▐▐ ■■■■■■■■■■■■ ▐▐▐ Page 11 of 20

6. Do you owe any overdue Federal, state, or local taxes? ☐ Yes ☒ No

7. A. Have you **EVER** not filed a Federal, state, or local tax return since you became a lawful permanent resident? ☐ Yes ☒ No

   B. If you answered "Yes," did you consider yourself to be a "non-U.S. resident"? ☐ Yes ☐ No

8. Have you called yourself a "non-U.S. resident" on a Federal, state, or local tax return since you became a lawful permanent resident? ☐ Yes ☒ No

9. A. Have you **EVER** been a member of, involved in, or in any way associated with, any organization, association, fund, foundation, party, club, society, or similar group in the United States or in any other location in the world? ☐ Yes ☒ No

   B. If you answered "Yes," provide the information below. If you need extra space, attach the names of the other groups on additional sheets of paper and provide any evidence to support your answers.

Name of the Group	Purpose of the Group	Dates of Membership	
		From (mm/dd/yyyy)	To (mm/dd/yyyy)

10. Have you **EVER** been a member of, or in any way associated (either directly or indirectly) with:

    A. The Communist Party? ☐ Yes ☒ No

    B. Any other totalitarian party? ☐ Yes ☒ No

    C. A terrorist organization? ☐ Yes ☒ No

11. Have you **EVER** advocated (either directly or indirectly) the overthrow of any government by force or violence? ☐ Yes ☒ No

12. Have you **EVER** persecuted (either directly or indirectly) any person because of race, religion, national origin, membership in a particular social group, or political opinion? ☐ Yes ☒ No

13. Between March 23, 1933 and May 8, 1945, did you work for or associate in any way (either directly or indirectly) with:

    A. The Nazi government of Germany? ☐ Yes ☒ No

    B. Any government in any area occupied by, allied with, or established with the help of the Nazi government of Germany? ☐ Yes ☒ No

    C. Any German, Nazi, or S.S. military unit, paramilitary unit, self-defense unit, vigilante unit, citizen unit, police unit, government agency or office, extermination camp, concentration camp, prisoner of war camp, prison, labor camp, or transit camp? ☐ Yes ☒ No

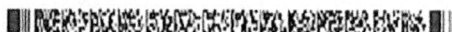

Part 12. Additional Information About You (Person Applying for Naturalization) (continued)   A-▬▬▬▬▬

14. Were you **EVER** involved in any way with any of the following:

    A. Genocide? ☐ Yes ☒ No

    B. Torture? ☐ Yes ☒ No

    C. Killing, or trying to kill, someone? ☐ Yes ☒ No

    D. Badly hurting, or trying to hurt, a person on purpose? ☐ Yes ☒ No

    E. Forcing, or trying to force, someone to have any kind of sexual contact or relations? ☐ Yes ☒ No

    F. Not letting someone practice his or her religion? ☐ Yes ☒ No

15. Were you **EVER** a member of, or did you **EVER** serve in, help, or otherwise participate in, any of the following groups:

    A. Military unit? ☐ Yes ☒ No

    B. Paramilitary unit (a group of people who act like a military group but are not part of the official military)? ☐ Yes ☒ No

    C. Police unit? ☐ Yes ☒ No

    D. Self-defense unit? ☐ Yes ☒ No

    E. Vigilante unit (a group of people who act like the police, but are not part of the official police)? ☐ Yes ☒ No

    F. Rebel group? ☐ Yes ☒ No

    G. Guerrilla group (a group of people who use weapons against or otherwise physically attack the military, police, government, or other people)? ☐ Yes ☒ No

    H. Militia (an army of people, not part of the official military)? ☐ Yes ☒ No

    I. Insurgent organization (a group that uses weapons and fights against a government)? ☐ Yes ☒ No

16. Were you **EVER** a worker, volunteer, or soldier, or did you otherwise **EVER** serve in any of the following:

    A. Prison or jail? ☐ Yes ☒ No

    B. Prison camp? ☐ Yes ☒ No

    C. Detention facility (a place where people are forced to stay)? ☐ Yes ☒ No

    D. Labor camp (a place where people are forced to work)? ☐ Yes ☒ No

    E. Any other place where people were forced to stay? ☐ Yes ☒ No

17. Were you **EVER** a part of any group, or did you **EVER** help any group, unit, or organization that used a weapon against any person, or threatened to do so? ☐ Yes ☒ No

    A. If you answered "Yes," when you were part of this group, or when you helped this group, did you ever use a weapon against another person? ☐ Yes ☐ No

    B. If you answered "Yes," when you were part of this group, or when you helped this group, did you ever tell another person that you would use a weapon against that person? ☐ Yes ☐ No

18. Did you **EVER** sell, give, or provide weapons to any person, or help another person sell, give, or provide weapons to any person? ☐ Yes ☒ No

    A. If you answered "Yes," did you know that this person was going to use the weapons against another person? ☐ Yes ☐ No

    B. If you answered "Yes," did you know that this person was going to sell or give the weapons to someone who was going to use them against another person? ☐ Yes ☐ No

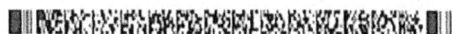

Part 12. Additional Information About You (Person Applying for Naturalization) (continued)

A- ▓▓▓▓▓▓▓▓▓

19. Did you EVER receive any type of military, paramilitary (a group of people who act like a military group but are not part of the official military), or weapons training? ☐ Yes ☒ No

20. Did you EVER recruit (ask), enlist (sign up), conscript (require), or use any person under 15 years of age to serve in or help an armed force or group? ☐ Yes ☒ No

21. Did you EVER use any person under 15 years of age to do anything that helped or supported people in combat? ☐ Yes ☒ No

If any of Item Numbers 22. - 28. apply to you, you must answer "Yes" even if your records have been sealed, expunged, or otherwise cleared. You must disclose this information even if someone, including a judge, law enforcement officer, or attorney, told you that it no longer constitutes a record or told you that you do not have to disclose the information.

22. Have you EVER committed, assisted in committing, or attempted to commit, a crime or offense for which you were NOT arrested? ☐ Yes ☒ No

23. Have you EVER been arrested, cited, or detained by any law enforcement officer (including any immigration official or any official of the U.S. armed forces) for any reason? ☒ Yes ☐ No

24. Have you EVER been charged with committing, attempting to commit, or assisting in committing a crime or offense? ☒ Yes ☐ No

25. Have you EVER been convicted of a crime or offense? ☒ Yes ☐ No

26. Have you EVER been placed in an alternative sentencing or a rehabilitative program (for example, diversion, deferred prosecution, withheld adjudication, deferred adjudication)? ☐ Yes ☒ No

27. A. Have you EVER received a suspended sentence, been placed on probation, or been paroled? ☒ Yes ☐ No

    B. If you answered "Yes," have you completed the probation or parole? ☒ Yes ☐ No

28. A. Have you EVER been in jail or prison? ☒ Yes ☐ No

    B. If you answered "Yes," how long were you in jail or prison? Years 0   Months 0   Days 1

29. If you answered "No" to ALL questions in Item Numbers 23. - 28., then skip this item and go to Item Number 30.

    If you answered "Yes" to any question in Item Numbers 23. - 28., then complete this table. If you need extra space, use additional sheets of paper and provide any evidence to support your answers.

Why were you arrested, cited, detained, or charged?	Date arrested, cited, detained, or charged. (mm/dd/yyyy)	Where were you arrested, cited, detained, or charged? (City or Town, State, Country)	Outcome or disposition of the arrest, citation, detention, or charge (no charges filed, charges dismissed, jail, probation, etc.)
VC § 23152(b)	11/10/2008	Downey, CA	36 Months Probation/Fine

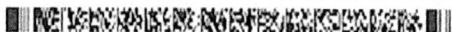

Answer **Item Numbers 30. - 46.** If you answer "Yes" to any of these questions, except **Item Numbers 37.** and **38.**, include a typed or printed explanation on additional sheets of paper and provide any evidence to support your answers.

30. Have you **EVER**:

    A. Been a habitual drunkard? ☐ Yes ☒ No

    B. Been a prostitute, or procured anyone for prostitution? ☐ Yes ☒ No

    C. Sold or smuggled controlled substances, illegal drugs, or narcotics? ☐ Yes ☒ No

    D. Been married to more than one person at the same time? ☐ Yes ☒ No

    E. Married someone in order to obtain an immigration benefit? ☐ Yes ☒ No

    F. Helped anyone to enter, or try to enter, the United States illegally? ☐ Yes ☒ No

    G. Gambled illegally or received income from illegal gambling? ☐ Yes ☒ No

    H. Failed to support your dependents or to pay alimony? ☐ Yes ☒ No

    I. Made any misrepresentation to obtain any public benefit in the United States? ☐ Yes ☒ No

31. Have you **EVER** given any U.S. Government officials **any** information or documentation that was false, fraudulent, or misleading? ☐ Yes ☒ No

32. Have you **EVER** lied to any U.S. Government officials to gain entry or admission into the United States or to gain immigration benefits while in the United States? ☐ Yes ☒ No

33. Have you **EVER** been removed, excluded, or deported from the United States? ☐ Yes ☒ No

34. Have you **EVER** been ordered removed, excluded, or deported from the United States? ☐ Yes ☒ No

35. Have you **EVER** been placed in removal, exclusion, rescission, or deportation proceedings? ☐ Yes ☒ No

36. Are removal, exclusion, rescission, or deportation proceedings (including administratively closed proceedings) **currently** pending against you? ☐ Yes ☒ No

37. Have you **EVER** served in the U.S. armed forces? ☐ Yes ☒ No

38. A. Are you **currently** a member of the U.S. armed forces? ☐ Yes ☒ No

    B. If you answered "Yes," are you scheduled to deploy overseas, including to a vessel, within the next three months? (Refer to the **Address Change** section in the Instructions on how to notify USCIS if you learn of your deployment plans after you file your Form N-400.) ☐ Yes ☐ No

    C. If you answered "Yes," are you **currently** stationed overseas? ☐ Yes ☐ No

39. Have you **EVER** been court-martialed, administratively separated, or disciplined, or have you received an other than honorable discharge, while in the U.S. armed forces? ☐ Yes ☒ No

40. Have you **EVER** been discharged from training or service in the U.S. armed forces because you were an alien? ☐ Yes ☒ No

41. Have you **EVER** left the United States to avoid being drafted in the U.S. armed forces? ☐ Yes ☒ No

42. Have you **EVER** applied for any kind of exemption from military service in the U.S. armed forces? ☐ Yes ☒ No

43. Have you **EVER** deserted from the U.S. armed forces? ☐ Yes ☒ No

44. A. Are you a male who lived in the United States at any time between your 18th and 26th birthdays? ☐ Yes ☒ No
(This does not include living in the United States as a lawful nonimmigrant.)

B. If you answered "Yes," when did you register for the Selective Service? Provide the information below.

Date Registered (mm/dd/yyyy)	Selective Service Number

C. If you answered "Yes," but you **did not register** with the Selective Service System and you are:

1. Still under 26 years of age, you must register before you apply for naturalization, and complete the Selective Service information above; OR

2. Now 26 to 31 years of age (29 years of age if you are filing under INA section 319(a)), but you did not register with the Selective Service, you must attach a statement explaining why you did not register, and provide a status information letter from the Selective Service.

Answer **Item Numbers 45. - 50.** If you answer "No" to any of these questions, include a typed or printed explanation on additional sheets of paper and provide any evidence to support your answers.

45. Do you support the Constitution and form of Government of the United States? ☒ Yes ☐ No

46. Do you understand the full Oath of Allegiance to the United States? ☒ Yes ☐ No

47. Are you willing to take the full Oath of Allegiance to the United States? ☒ Yes ☐ No

48. If the law requires it, are you willing to bear arms on behalf of the United States? ☒ Yes ☐ No

49. If the law requires it, are you willing to perform noncombatant services in the U.S. armed forces? ☒ Yes ☐ No

50. If the law requires it, are you willing to perform work of national importance under civilian direction? ☒ Yes ☐ No

Part 13. Applicant's Statement, Certification, and Signature

NOTE: Read the **Penalties** section of the Form N-400 Instructions before completing this part.

Applicant's Statement

NOTE: Select the box for either **Item A.** or **B.** in **Item Number 1.** If applicable, select the box for **Item Number 2.**

1. Applicant's Statement Regarding the Interpreter

   A. ☒ I can read and understand English, and I have read and understand every question and instruction on this application and my answer to every question.

   B. ☐ The interpreter named in **Part 14.** read to me every question and instruction on this application and my answer to every question in [blank] , a language in which I am fluent, and I understood everything.

2. Applicant's Statement Regarding the Preparer

   ☒ At my request, the preparer named in **Part 15.**, | Christopher A. Reed |
   prepared this application for me based only upon information I provided or authorized.

Part 13. Applicant's Statement, Certification, and Signature (continued)

A- 0 9 5 4 9 6 9 3 8

Applicant's Certification

Copies of any documents I have submitted are exact photocopies of unaltered, original documents, and I understand that USCIS may require that I submit original documents to USCIS at a later date. Furthermore, I authorize the release of any information from any of my records that USCIS may need to determine my eligibility for the immigration benefit that I seek.

I further authorize release of information contained in this application, in supporting documents, and in my USCIS records to other entities and persons where necessary for the administration and enforcement of U.S. immigration laws.

I understand that USCIS will require me to appear for an appointment to take my biometrics (fingerprints, photograph, and/or signature) and, at that time, I will be required to sign an oath reaffirming that:

1) I reviewed and provided or authorized all of the information in my application;

2) I understood all of the information contained in, and submitted with, my application; and

3) All of this information was complete, true, and correct at the time of filing.

I certify, under penalty of perjury, that I provided or authorized all of the information in my application, I understand all of the information contained in, and submitted with, my application, and that all of this information is complete, true, and correct.

Applicant's Signature

3. Applicant's Signature

⇨

Date of Signature (mm/dd/yyyy)

09/11/2020

NOTE TO ALL APPLICANTS: If you do not completely fill out this application or fail to submit required documents listed in the Instructions, USCIS may deny your application.

Part 14. Interpreter's Contact Information, Certification, and Signature

Provide the following information about the interpreter.

Interpreter's Full Name

1. Interpreter's Family Name (Last Name)   Interpreter's Given Name (First Name)

2. Interpreter's Business or Organization Name (if any)

Interpreter's Mailing Address

3. Street Number and Name   Apt. Ste. Flr. Number

City or Town   State   ZIP Code + 4

Province   Postal Code   Country

Part 14. Interpreter's Contact Information, Certification, and Signature (continued)

A- 0 9 5 4 9 6 9 3 8

Interpreter's Contact Information

4. Interpreter's Daytime Telephone Number

5. Interpreter's Mobile Telephone Number (if any)

6. Interpreter's Email Address (if any)

Interpreter's Certification

I certify, under penalty of perjury, that:

I am fluent in English and _____, which is the same language specified in **Part 13., Item B.** in **Item Number 1.**, and I have read to this applicant in the identified language every question and instruction on this application and his or her answer to every question. The applicant informed me that he or she understands every instruction, question and answer on the application, including the **Applicant's Certification** and has verified the accuracy of every answer.

Interpreter's Signature

7. Interpreter's Signature

Date of Signature (mm/dd/yyyy)

Part 15. Contact Information, Declaration, and Signature of the Person Preparing This Application, if Other Than the Applicant

Provide the following information about the preparer.

Preparer's Full Name

1. Preparer's Family Name (Last Name)

Reed

Preparer's Given Name (First Name)

Christopher

2. Preparer's Business or Organization Name (if any)

Law Offices of Brian D. Lerner, APC

Preparer's Mailing Address

3. Street Number and Name

3233 E. Broadway

Apt. Ste. Flr. Number

City or Town

Long Beach

State

CA

ZIP Code + 4

90803 -

Province

Postal Code

Country

USA

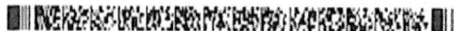

Part 15. Contact Information, Declaration, and Signature of the Person Preparing This Application, if Other Than the Applicant (continued)

A- | 0 | 9 | 5 | 4 | 9 | 6 | 9 | 3 | 8

Preparer's Contact Information

4. Preparer's Daytime Telephone Number

(562) 495-0554

5. Preparer's Mobile Telephone Number (if any)

N/A

6. Preparer's Email Address (if any)

creed@eimmigration.org

Preparer's Statement

7. A. ☐ I am not an attorney or accredited representative but have prepared this application on behalf of the applicant and with the applicant's consent.

B. ☒ I am an attorney or accredited representative and my representation of the applicant in this case ☒ extends ☐ does not extend beyond the preparation of this application.

NOTE: If you are an attorney or accredited representative whose representation extends beyond preparation of this application, you may be obliged to submit a completed Form G-28, Notice of Entry of Appearance as Attorney or Accredited Representative, with this application.

Preparer's Certification

By my signature, I certify, under penalty of perjury, that I prepared this application at the request of the applicant. The applicant then reviewed this completed application and informed me that he or she understands all of the information contained in, and submitted with, his or her application, including the **Applicant's Certification**, and that all of this information is complete, true, and correct. I completed this application based only on information that the applicant provided to me or authorized me to obtain or use.

Preparer's Signature

8. Preparer's Signature

➡ _(signature)_

Date of Signature (mm/dd/yyyy)

09/11/2020

NOTE: Do not complete Parts 16., 17., or 18. until the USCIS Officer instructs you to do so at the interview.

Part 16. Signature at Interview

I swear (affirm) and certify under penalty of perjury under the laws of the United States of America that I know that the contents of this Form N-400, Application for Naturalization, subscribed by me, including corrections number 1 through _____, are complete, true, and correct. The evidence submitted by me on numbered pages 1 through _____ are complete, true, and correct.

Subscribed to and sworn to (affirmed) before me

USCIS Officer's Printed Name or Stamp	Date of Signature (mm/dd/yyyy)

Applicant's Signature

USCIS Officer's Signature

Part 17. Renunciation of Foreign Titles

A- 0 9 5 4 9 6 9 3 8

If you answered "Yes" to **Part 12., Items A. and B.** in **Item Number 4.,** then you must affirm the following before a USCIS officer:

I further renounce the title of _____ **which I have heretofore held; or**
(list titles)

I further renounce the order of nobility of _____ **to which I have heretofore belonged.**
(list order of nobility)

Applicant's Printed Name

Applicant's Signature

USCIS Officer's Printed Name

USCIS Officer's Signature

Date of Signature (mm/dd/yyyy)

Part 18. Oath of Allegiance

If your application is approved, you will be scheduled for a public oath ceremony at which time you will be required to take the following Oath of Allegiance immediately prior to becoming a naturalized citizen. By signing below you acknowledge your willingness and ability to take this oath:

I hereby declare on oath, that I absolutely and entirely renounce and abjure all allegiance and fidelity to any foreign prince, potentate, state, or sovereignty, of whom or which I have heretofore been a subject or citizen;

that I will support and defend the Constitution and laws of the United States of America against all enemies, foreign, and domestic;

that I will bear true faith and allegiance to the same;

that I will bear arms on behalf of the United States when required by the law;

that I will perform noncombatant service in the armed forces of the United States when required by the law;

that I will perform work of national importance under civilian direction when required by the law; and

that I take this obligation freely, without any mental reservation or purpose of evasion; so help me God.

Applicant's Printed Name

Family Name (Last Name)	Given Name (First Name)	Middle Name (if applicable)

Applicant's Signature

Date of Signature (mm/dd/yyyy)

Addendum

HEREDIA CABRERA, Maria Alejandra, Form: N-400, A# 095496938 , 09/11/2020 (Page 1)

Part 11: Additional Children:

EXHIBITS

EXHIBIT '1':
Applicant's Permanent Resident Card

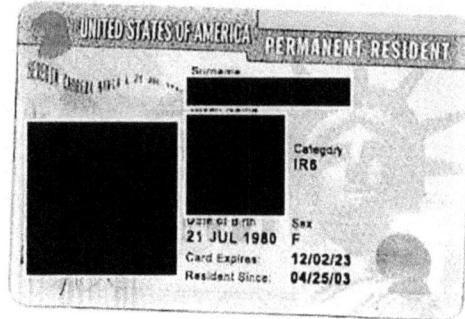

UNITED STATES OF AMERICA PERMANENT RESIDENT

Surname

Category
IR6

Date of Birth   Sex
21 JUL 1980   F
Card Expires: 12/02/23
Resident Since: 04/25/03

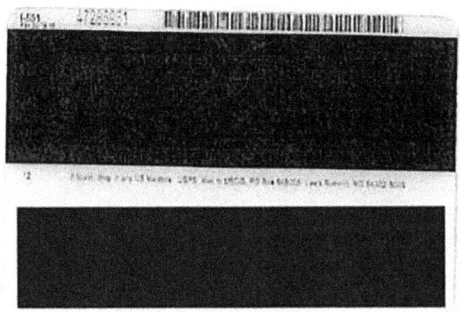

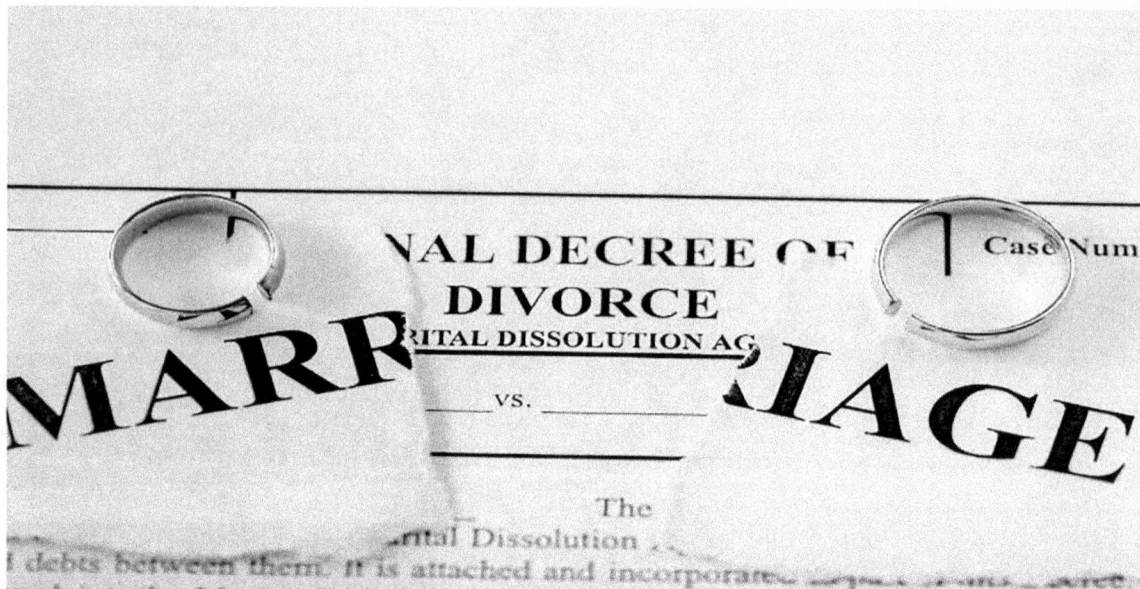

SUPERIOR COURT OF CALIFORNIA, COUNTY OF LOS ANGELES

Case Name:
Case Numbe

NOTICE OF DEFAULT SET FOR TRIAL

TO THE ABOVE NAMED PARTY OR YOUR ATTORNEY OF RECORD:

You are hereby notified that your matter has been set for default trial on 06-12-12 at 8:30 am, in DEPT. SO A [SOA] of the Superior Court, located at 415 West Ocean Blvd., Long Beach, California 90802.

Please be advised that, pursuant to California Rule of Court Rule 5.136 and Los Angeles Superior Court Rule 14.19, you must submit the following:

  (1) NOTICE OF ENTRY FORM FL-190
  (2) AN ORIGINAL JUDGMENT FORM (FL-180) PLUS THREE COPIES
  (3) DECLARATION FOR DEFAULT OR UNCONTESTED DISSOLUTION FORM FL-170.
  (4) DECLARATION REGARDING SERVICE OF PRELIMINARY DECLARATION OF DISCLOSURE. FORM FL-141.
  (5) DECLARATION REGARDING SERVICE OF FINAL DECLARATION OF DISCLOSURE FL-141 OR WAIVER AS INDICATED ON FL-170.
  (6) TWO STAMPED SELF-ADDRESSED ENVELOPES LEGAL SIZE 4x 9½" ADDRESSED TO THE PARTIES APPEARING IN THIS ACTION.

\FAILURE TO COMPLY WITH THESE RULES SHALL BE CAUSE FOR REFUSAL TO SIGN THE JUDGMENT.

If you are requesting a JUDGMENT OF PATERNITY, you must submit a PATERNITY JUDGMENT FORM (FL-250).

CLERK'S CERTIFICATE OF MAILING

I, the below-named Executive Officer/Clerk of the above-entitled court, do hereby certify that I am not a party to the cause herein, and that on this date I served the Notice of Default Set for Trial upon each party or counsel named above by depositing in the United States mail at the courthouse in Long Beach , California, one copy of the original filed/entered document in a separate sealed envelope to each address shown above with the postage thereon fully prepaid, in accordance with standard court practices.

Dated: April 27, 2012

JOHN A. CLARKE, Executive Officer/Clerk of the Superior Court of California, County of Los Angeles

By:_____Deputy

ATTORNEY OR PARTY WITHOUT ATTORNEY (Name, State Bar number, and address):

█████████████████████

TELEPHONE NO.: (562)507-8865   FAX NO. (Optional):
E-MAIL ADDRESS (Optional):
ATTORNEY FOR (Name): Self-Represented

FOR COURT USE ONLY

CONFORMED COPY
OF ORIGINAL FILED
Los Angeles Superior Court

JUN 1 2 2012

John A. Clarke, Executive Officer/Clerk
By_____
DEPUTY

SUPERIOR COURT OF CALIFORNIA, COUNTY OF LOS ANGELES
STREET ADDRESS: 415 West Ocean Boulevard
MAILING ADDRESS: same as above
CITY AND ZIP CODE: Long Beach, CA 90802
BRANCH NAME: SOUTH JUDICIAL DISTRICT

MARRIAGE OF

█████████████████████

JUDGMENT

[X] DISSOLUTION	[ ] LEGAL SEPARATION	[ ] NULLITY

[ ] Status only
[ ] Reserving jurisdiction over termination of marital or domestic partnership status
[ ] Judgment on reserved issues   JUN 12 2012
Date marital or domestic partnership status ends:

CASE NUMBER:

ND066521

1. [ ] This judgment [ ] contains personal conduct restraining orders [ ] modifies existing restraining orders.
   The restraining orders are contained on page(s)   of the attachment. They expire on (date):

2. This proceeding was heard as follows: [X] Default or uncontested [ ] By declaration under Family Code section 2336
   [ ] Contested
   a. Date: June 12, 2012   Dept.: A   Room: 41
   b. Judicial officer (name): LORI R. BEHAR   [X] Temporary judge
   c. [X] Petitioner present in court   [ ] Attorney present in court (name):
   d. [ ] Respondent present in court   [ ] Attorney present in court (name):
   e. [ ] Claimant present in court (name):   [ ] Attorney present in court (name):
   f. [ ] Other (specify name):

3. The court acquired jurisdiction of the respondent on (date): 6/8/2011
   a. [X] The respondent was served with process.
   b. [ ] The respondent appeared.

THE COURT ORDERS, GOOD CAUSE APPEARING

4. a. [X] Judgment of dissolution is entered. Marital or domestic partnership status is terminated and the parties are restored to the status of single persons   JUN 12 2012
      (1) [X] on (specify date):
      (2) [ ] on a date to be determined on noticed motion of either party or on stipulation.
   b. [ ] Judgment of legal separation is entered.
   c. [ ] Judgment of nullity is entered. The parties are declared to be single persons on the ground of (specify):

   d. [ ] This judgment will be entered nunc pro tunc as of (date):
   e. [ ] Judgment on reserved issues.
   f. The [X] petitioner's [ ] respondent's former name is restored to (specify): MARIA A. HEREDIA RAMIREZ
   g. [ ] Jurisdiction is reserved over all other issues, and all present orders remain in effect except as provided below.
   h. [ ] This judgment contains provisions for child support or family support. Each party must complete and file with the court a Child Support Case Registry Form (form FL-191) within 10 days of the date of this judgment. The parents must notify the court of any change in the information submitted within 10 days of the change, by filing an updated form. The Notice of Rights and Responsibilities—Health Care Costs and Reimbursement Procedures and Information Sheet on Changing a Child Support Order (form FL-192) is attached.

Page 1 of 2

Form Adopted for Mandatory Use
Judicial Council of California
FL-180 [Rev. January 1. 2007]

JUDGMENT
(Family Law)

Legal Solutions Plus

Family Code §§ 2024, 2340, 2343, 2346

Office of the Family Law Facilitator.

1 of 12

CASE NAME (Last name, first name of each party): In re CABRERA, MARIA A. and ANDY D.	CASE NUMBER ND066521

4. *(Cont'd.)*

i. [ ] A settlement agreement between the parties is attached.

j. [ ] A written stipulation for judgment between the parties is attached.

k. [X] The children of this marriage or domestic partnership.

    (1) [X] The children of this marriage or domestic partnership are:

Name	Birthdate
▮▮▮▮▮▮▮▮	5/15/1999
	10/20/2000
▮▮▮▮▮▮▮▮	1/11/2003

    (2) [X] Parentage is established for children of this relationship born prior to the marriage or domestic partnership.

l. [X] Child custody and visitation are ordered as set forth in the attached

    (1) [ ] settlement agreement, stipulation for judgment, or other written agreement.

    (2) [X] *Child Custody and Visitation Order Attachment* (form FL-341).

    (3) [ ] *Stipulation and Order for Custody and/or Visitation of Children* (form FL-355).

    (4) [ ] other *(specify)*:

m. [X] Child support is ordered as set forth in the attached

    (1) [ ] settlement agreement, stipulation for judgment, or other written agreement.

    (2) [X] *Child Support Information and Order Attachment* (form FL-342).

    (3) [ ] *Stipulation to Establish or Modify Child Support and Order* (form FL-350).

    (4) [ ] other *(specify)*:

n. [X] Spousal or partner support is ordered as set forth in the attached

    (1) [ ] settlement agreement, stipulation for judgment, or other written agreement.

    (2) [X] *Spousal, Partner, or Family Support Order Attachment* (form FL-343).

    (3) [ ] other *(specify)*:

NOTICE: It is the goal of this state that each party will make reasonable good faith efforts to become self-supporting as provided for in Family Code section 4320. The failure to make reasonable good faith efforts may be one of the factors considered by the court as a basis for modifying or terminating spousal or partner support.

o. [X] Property division is ordered as set forth in the attached

    (1) [ ] settlement agreement, stipulation for judgment, or other written agreement.

    (2) [X] *Property Order Attachment to Judgment* (form FL-345).

    (3) [ ] other *(specify)*:

p. [ ] Other *(specify)*:

Each attachment to this judgment is incorporated into this judgment and the parties are ordered to comply with each attachment's provisions.

Jurisdiction is reserved to make other orders necessary to carry out this judgment.

Date: **JUN 1 2 2012**

Commr. L. Beh

JUDICIAL OF **COMMR. LORI R. BEHAR**

[ ] SIGNATURE FOLLOWS LAST ATTACHMENT

5. Number of pages attached: ___10___

NOTICE

Dissolution or legal separation may automatically cancel the rights of a spouse or domestic partner under the other spouse's or domestic partner's will, trust, retirement plan, power of attorney, pay-on-death bank account, transfer-on-death vehicle registration, survivorship rights to any property owned in joint tenancy, and any other similar thing. It does not automatically cancel the rights of a spouse or domestic partner as beneficiary of the other spouse's or domestic partner's life insurance policy. You should review these matters, as well as any credit cards, other credit accounts, insurance policies, retirement plans, and credit reports, to determine whether they should be changed or whether you should take any other actions.

A debt or obligation may be assigned to one party as part of the dissolution of property and debts, but if that party does not pay the debt or obligation, the creditor may be able to collect from the other party.

An earnings assignment may be issued without additional proof if child, family, partner, or spousal support is ordered.

Any party required to pay support must pay interest on overdue amounts at the "legal rate," which is currently 10 percent.

FL-180 [Rev. January 1, 2007]

JUDGMENT
(Family Law)

Page 2 of 2

2 of 12

PETITIONER/PLAINTIFF:	██████████████	CASE NUMBER
RESPONDENT/DEFENDANT:	██████████████	ND066521

CHILD CUSTODY AND VISITATION ORDER ATTACHMENT

TO   [ ] *Findings and Order After Hearing*   [X] *Judgment*

      [ ] *Stipulation and Order for Custody and/or Visitation of Children*

      [ ] *Other (specify):*

1. [X] **Custody.** Custody of the minor children of the parties is awarded as follows:

Child's name	Date of birth	Legal custody to (person who makes decisions about health, education, etc.)	Physical custody to (person with whom the child lives)
████████████████████ ████████████████████ ████████████████████		Sole Legal Custody of the minor children is awarded to Petitioner MARIA A. CABRERA	Sole Physical Custody of the minor children is awarded to Petitioner MARIA A. CABRERA

2. [X] **Visitation**

   a. [ ] Reasonable right of visitation to the party without physical custody (not appropriate in cases involving domestic violence)

   b. [ ] See the attached _____ -page document dated (specify date):

   c. [ ] The parties will go to mediation at (specify location):

   d. [X] No visitation

   e. [X] Visitation for the [ ] petitioner [X] respondent will be as follows:

     (1) [ ] Weekends starting (date):

       (The first weekend of the month is the first weekend with a Saturday.)

       [ ] 1st [ ] 2nd [ ] 3rd [ ] 4th [ ] 5th weekend of the month

       from _____ at _____ [ ] a.m. [ ] p.m.
           (day of week)   (time)

       to _____ at _____ [ ] a.m. [ ] p.m.
           (day of week)   (time)

       (a) [ ] The parents will alternate the fifth weekends, with the [ ] petitioner [ ] respondent having the initial fifth weekend, which starts (date):

       (b) [ ] The petitioner will have fifth weekends in [ ] odd [ ] even months.

     (2) [ ] Alternate weekends starting (date):

       The [ ] petitioner [ ] respondent will have the children with him or her during the period

       from _____ at _____ [ ] a.m. [ ] p.m.
           (day of week)   (time)

       to _____ at _____ [ ] a.m. [ ] p.m.
           (day of week)   (time)

     (3) [ ] Weekdays starting (date):

       The [ ] petitioner [ ] respondent will have the children with him or her during the period

       from _____ at _____ [ ] a.m. [ ] p.m.
           (day of week)   (time)

       to _____ at _____ [ ] a.m. [ ] p.m.
           (day of week)   (time)

     (4) [X] Other (specify days and times as well as any additional restrictions): In the event Respondent wishes to visit the children, Respondent may make an appropriate application to the Court for consideration.

                              [ ] See Attachment 2e(4).

Form Approved for Optional Use
Judicial Council of California
FL-341 [Rev. July 1, 2008]

CHILD CUSTODY AND VISITATION ORDER ATTACHMENT

Legal Solutions Plus

Page 1 of 2

Family Code §§ 3011, 3022, 3025, 3040-3043, 3048, 3100-3140, 7604

3:/12

PETITIONER/PLAINTIFF		CASE NUMBER
RESPONDENT/DEFENDANT		ND066521

3. ☐ The court acknowledges that criminal protective orders in case number (specify):
in (specify court): relating to the parties in this case are in effect under Penal Code section 136.2, are current, and have priority of enforcement.

4. ☐ Supervised visitation. Until ☐ further order of the court ☐ other (specify):
the ☐ petitioner ☐ respondent will have supervised visitation with the minor children according to the schedule set forth on page 1. **(You must attach form FL-341(A).)**

5. ☐ Transportation for visitation
   a. ☐ Transportation to the visits will be provided by the ☐ petitioner ☐ respondent
       ☐ other (specify):
   b. ☐ Transportation from the visits will be provided by the ☐ petitioner ☐ respondent
       ☐ other (specify):
   c. ☐ Drop-off of the children will be at (address):
   d. ☐ Pick-up of the children will be at (address):
   e. ☐ The children will be driven only by a licensed and insured driver. The car or truck must have legal child restraint devices.
   f. ☐ During the exchanges, the parent driving the children will wait in the car and the other parent will wait in his or her home while the children go between the car and the home.
   g. ☐ Other (specify):

6. ☐ Travel with children. The ☐ petitioner ☐ respondent ☐ other (name):
must have written permission from the other parent or a court order to take the children out of
   a. ☐ the state of California.
   b. ☐ the following counties (specify):
   c. ☐ other places (specify):

7. ☐ Child abduction prevention. There is a risk that one of the parents will take the children out of California without the other parent's permission. Form FL-341(B) is attached and must be obeyed.

8. ☐ Holiday schedule. The children will spend holiday time as listed in the attached ☐ form FL-341(C)
   ☐ other (specify):

9. ☐ Additional custody provisions. The parents will follow the additional custody provisions listed in the attached
   ☐ form FL-341(D) ☐ other (specify):

10. ☐ Joint legal custody. The parents will share joint legal custody as listed in the attached ☐ form FL-341(E)
   ☐ other (specify):

11. ☐ Other (specify):

12. Jurisdiction. This court has jurisdiction to make child custody orders in this case under the Uniform Child Custody Jurisdiction and Enforcement Act (part 3 of the California Family Code, commencing with section 3400).

13. Notice and opportunity to be heard. The responding party was given notice and an opportunity to be heard, as provided by the laws of the State of California.

14. Country of habitual residence. The country of habitual residence of the child or children in this case is
   [X] the United States ☐ other (specify):

15. Penalties for violating this order. If you violate this order, you may be subject to civil or criminal penalties, or both.

FL-341 [Rev. July 1, 2006]   **CHILD CUSTODY AND VISITATION ORDER ATTACHMENT**   Page 2 of 2

4/6/12

PETITIONER/PLAINTIFF ▮

RESPONDENT/DEFENDANT: ▮

OTHER PARENT:

CASE NUMBER

ND066521

CHILD SUPPORT INFORMATION AND ORDER ATTACHMENT

Attachment to ☐ Findings and Order After Hearing ☐ Restraining Order After Hearing (CLETS)

☒ Judgment ☐ Other

THE COURT USED THE FOLLOWING INFORMATION IN DETERMINING THE AMOUNT OF CHILD SUPPORT:

1. ☐ A printout of a computer calculation and findings is attached and incorporated in this order for all required items not filled out below.

2. ☐ Income

   a. Each parent's monthly income is as follows:

	Gross monthly income	Net monthly income	Receiving TANF/CalWORKS
Petitioner/plaintiff:	$	$	☐
Respondent/defendant:	$	$	☐
Other parent:	$	$	☐

   b. Imputation of income. The court finds that the ☐ petitioner/plaintiff ☐ respondent/defendant ☐ other parent has the capacity to earn:

   $ _____ per _____ and has based the support order upon this imputed income.

3. ☒ Children of this relationship

   a. Number of children who are the subjects of the support order (specify): Three (3)

   b. Approximate percentage of time spent with petitioner/plaintiff: _____ %
   respondent/defendant: _____ %
   other parent: _____ %

4. ☐ Hardships

   Hardships for the following have been allowed in calculating child support:

	Petitioner/plaintiff	Respondent/defendant	Other parent	Approximate ending time for the hardship
a. ☐ Other minor children:	$	$	$	
b. ☐ Extraordinary medical expenses:	$	$	$	
c. ☐ Catastrophic losses:	$	$	$	

THE COURT ORDERS

5. ☐ Low-income adjustment

   a. ☐ The low-income adjustment applies.

   b. ☐ The low-income adjustment does not apply because (specify reasons):

6. ☒ Child support SEE #12 NEXT PAGE

   a. Base child support

   ☐ Petitioner/plaintiff ☐ Respondent/defendant ☐ Other parent must pay child support beginning (date): _____ and continuing until further order of the court, or until the child marries, dies, is emancipated, reaches age 19, or reaches age 18 and is not a full-time high school student, whichever occurs first, as follows:

Child's name	Date of birth	Monthly amount	Payable to (name):
▮		SEE #12 NEXT PAGE	
▮		SEE #12 NEXT PAGE	
▮		SEE #12 NEXT PAGE	

   Payable ☐ on the 1st of the month ☐ one-half on the 1st and one-half on the 15th of the month
   ☐ other (specify):

   b. ☐ Mandatory additional child support

   (1) ☐ Child-care costs related to employment or reasonably necessary job training

   (a) ☐ Petitioner/plaintiff must pay: _____ % of total or ☐ $ _____ per month child-care costs.

   (b) ☐ Respondent/defendant must pay: _____ % of total or ☐ $ _____ per month child-care costs.

   (c) ☐ Other parent must pay: _____ % of total or ☐ $ _____ per month child-care costs.

   (d) ☐ Costs to be paid as follows (specify):

THIS IS A COURT ORDER.

Form Adopted for Mandatory Use
Judicial Council of California
FL-342 [Rev. January 1, 2010]

CHILD SUPPORT INFORMATION AND ORDER ATTACHMENT

Legal Solutions Plus

PETITIONER/PLAINTIFF:	████████	CASE NUMBER
RESPONDENT/DEFENDANT:	████████	
OTHER PARENT:	████████	ND066521

THE COURT FURTHER ORDERS

6. b. **Mandatory additional child support**

 (2) [X] Reasonable uninsured health-care costs for the children

    (a) [X] Petitioner/plaintiff must pay: 50.00 % of total or [ ] $ per month.

    (b) [X] Respondent/defendant must pay: 50.0 % of total or [ ] $ per month.

    (c) [ ] Other parent must pay: % of total or [ ] $ per month.

    (d) [ ] Costs to be paid as follows (specify):

 c. [ ] **Additional child support**

    (1) [ ] Costs related to the educational or other special needs of the children

      (a) [ ] Petitioner/plaintiff must pay: % of total or [ ] $ per month.

      (b) [ ] Respondent/defendant must pay: % of total or [ ] $ per month.

      (c) [ ] Other parent must pay: % of total or [ ] $ per month.

      (d) [ ] Costs to be paid as follows (specify):

    (2) [ ] Travel expenses for visitation

      (a) [ ] Petitioner/plaintiff must pay: % of total or [ ] $ per month.

      (b) [ ] Respondent/defendant must pay: % of total or [ ] $ per month.

      (c) [ ] Other parent must pay: % of total or [ ] $ per month.

      (d) [ ] Costs to be paid as follows (specify):

> Total child support per month: $ SEE #12 BELOW

7. **Health-Care Expenses**

 a. Health insurance coverage for the minor children of the parties must be maintained by the [X] petitioner/plaintiff [X] respondent/defendant [ ] other parent if available at no or reasonable cost through their respective places of employment or self-employment. Both parties are ordered to cooperate in the presentation, collection, and reimbursement of any health-care claims. The parent ordered to provide health insurance must seek continuation of coverage for the child after the child attains the age when the child is no longer considered eligible for coverage as a dependent under the insurance contract, if the child is incapable of self-sustaining employment because of a physically or mentally disabling injury, illness, or condition and is chiefly dependent upon the parent providing health insurance for support and maintenance.

 b. [ ] Health insurance is not available to the [ ] petitioner/plaintiff [ ] respondent/defendant [ ] other parent at a reasonable cost at this time.

 c. [ ] The party providing coverage must assign the right of reimbursement to the other party.

8. **Earnings Assignment**

 An earnings assignment order is issued. Note: The payor of child support is responsible for the payment of support directly to the recipient until support payments are deducted from the payor's wages and for payment of any support not paid by the assignment.

9. In the event that there is a contract between a party receiving support and a private child support collector, the party ordered to pay support must pay the fee charged by the private child support collector. This fee must not exceed 33 1/3 percent of the total amount of past due support nor may it exceed 50 percent of any fee charged by the private child support collector. The money judgment created by this provision is in favor of the private child support collector and the party receiving support, jointly.

10. [ ] **Non-Guideline Order**

 This order does not meet the child support guideline set forth in Family Code section 4055. A *Non-Guideline Child Support Findings Attachment* (form FL-342(A)) is attached.

11. [ ] **Employment Search Order (Family Code, § 4505)**

 [ ] Petitioner/plaintiff [ ] Respondent/defendant [ ] Other parent is ordered to seek employment with the following terms and conditions:

12. **Other Orders** (specify): The Court notes 2 pending Child Support Services Dept. cases BY545716 & BY483178. This Court defers jurisdiction over the issue of child support to the pending Child Support Services Dept. cases

13. **Required Attachments** until such time as it is properly brought before this Court.

 A *Notice of Rights and Responsibilities (Health-Care Costs and Reimbursement Procedures)* and *Information Sheet on Changing a Child Support Order* (form FL-192) must be attached and is incorporated into this order.

14. **Child Support Case Registry Form**

 Both parties must complete and file with the court a *Child Support Case Registry Form* (form FL-191) within 10 days of the date of this order. Thereafter, the parties must notify the court of any change in the information submitted within 10 days of the change by filing an updated form.

> **NOTICE:** Any party required to pay child support must pay interest on overdue amounts at the legal rate, which is currently 10 percent per year.

THIS IS A COURT ORDER.

FL-342 [Rev. January 1, 2010]   **CHILD SUPPORT INFORMATION AND ORDER ATTACHMENT**   Page 2 of 2

IF YOU HAVE A CHILD SUPPORT ORDER THAT INCLUDES A PROVISION FOR THE REIMBURSEMENT OF A PORTION OF THE CHILD'S OR CHILDREN'S HEALTH-CARE COSTS AND THOSE COSTS ARE NOT PAID BY INSURANCE, THE LAW SAYS:

1. Notice. You must give the other parent an itemized statement of the charges that have been billed for any health-care costs not paid by insurance. You must give this statement to the other parent within a reasonable time, but no more than 30 days after those costs were given to you.

2. Proof of full payment. If you have already paid all of the uninsured costs, you must (1) give the other parent proof that you paid them and (2) ask for reimbursement for the other parent's court-ordered share of those costs.

3. Proof of partial payment. If you have paid only your share of the uninsured costs, you must (1) give the other parent proof that you paid your share, (2) ask that the other parent pay his or her share of the costs directly to the health-care provider, and (3) give the other parent the information necessary for that parent to be able to pay the bill.

4. Payment by notified parent. If you receive notice from a parent that an uninsured health-care cost has been incurred, you must pay your share of that cost within the time the court orders; or if the court has not specified a period of time, you must make payment (1) within 30 days from the time you were given notice of the amount due, (2) according to any payment schedule set by the health-care provider, (3) according to a schedule agreed to in writing by you and the other parent, or (4) according to a schedule adopted by the court.

5. Disputed charges. If you dispute a charge, you may file a motion in court to resolve the dispute, but only if you pay that charge before filing your motion.

If you claim that the other party has failed to reimburse you for a payment, or the other party has failed to make a payment to the provider after proper notice has been given, you may file a motion in court to resolve the dispute. The court will presume that if uninsured costs have been paid, those costs were reasonable. The court may award attorney fees and costs against a party who has been unreasonable.

6. Court-ordered insurance coverage. If a parent provides health-care insurance as ordered by the court, that insurance must be used at all times to the extent that it is available for health-care costs.

a. **Burden to prove.** The party claiming that the coverage is inadequate to meet the child's needs has the burden of proving that to the court.

b. **Cost of additional coverage.** If a parent purchases health-care insurance in addition to that ordered by the court, that parent must pay all the costs of the additional coverage. In addition, if a parent uses alternative coverage that costs more than the coverage provided by court order, that parent must pay the difference.

7. Preferred health providers. If the court-ordered coverage designates a preferred health-care provider, that provider must be used at all times consistent with the terms of the health insurance policy. When any party uses a health-care provider other than the preferred provider, any health-care costs that would have been paid by the preferred health provider if that provider had been used must be the sole responsibility of the party incurring those costs.

Form Approved for Optional Use
Judicial Council of California
FL-192 [Rev. July 1 2007]

NOTICE OF RIGHTS AND RESPONSIBILITIES
Health-Care Costs and Reimbursement Procedures

Legal
Solutions
& Plus

Page 1 of 2

Family Code §§ 4063, 4064

INFORMATION SHEET ON CHANGING A CHILD SUPPORT ORDER

FL-192

General Information

The court has just made a child support order in your case. This order will remain the same unless a party to the action requests that the support be changed (modified). An order for child support can be modified only by filing a motion to change child support and serving each party involved in your case. If both parents and the local child support agency (if it is involved) agree on a new child support amount, you can complete, have all parties sign, and file with the court a *Stipulation to Establish or Modify Child Support and Order* (form FL-350) or *Stipulation and Order (Governmental)* (form FL-625).

When a Child Support Order May Be Modified

The court takes several things into account when ordering the payment of child support. First, the number of children is considered. Next, the net incomes of both parents are determined, along with the percentage of time each parent has physical custody of the children. The court considers both parties' tax filing status and may consider hardships, such as a child of another relationship. An existing order for child support may be modified when the net income of one of the parents changes significantly, the parenting schedule changes significantly, or a new child is born.

Examples

- You have been ordered to pay $500 per month in child support. You lose your job. You will continue to owe $500 per month, plus 10 percent interest on any unpaid support, unless you file a motion to modify your child support to a lower amount and the court orders a reduction.
- You are currently receiving $300 per month in child support from the other parent, whose net income has just increased substantially. You will continue to receive $300 per month unless you file a motion to modify your child support to a higher amount and the court orders an increase.
- You are paying child support based upon having physical custody of your children 30 percent of the time. After several months it turns out that you actually have physical custody of the children 50 percent of the time. You may file a motion to modify child support to a lower amount.

How to Change a Child Support Order

To change a child support order, you must file papers with the court. *Remember:* You must follow the order you have now.

What forms do I need?

If you are asking to change a child support order open with the local child support agency, you must fill out one of these forms:
- FL-680, *Notice of Motion (Governmental)* or FL-683 *Order to Show Cause (Governmental)* and
- FL-684, *Request for Order and Supporting Declaration (Governmental)*

If you are asking to change a child support order that is not open with the local child support agency, you must fill out one of these forms:
- FL-301, *Notice of Motion* or FL-300, *Order to Show Cause* and
- FL-310, *Application for Order and Supporting Declaration* or
- FL-390, *Notice of Motion and Motion for Simplified Modification of Order for Child, Spousal, or Family Support*

You must also fill out one of these forms:
- FL-150, *Income and Expense Declaration* or FL-155, *Financial Statement (Simplified)*

What if I am not sure which forms to fill out?

Talk to the family law facilitator at your court.

After you fill out the forms, file them with the court clerk and ask for a hearing date. Write the hearing date on the form. The clerk will ask you to pay a filing fee. If you cannot afford the fee, fill out these forms, too:
- Form FW-001, *Application for Waiver of Court Fees and Costs*
- Form FW-003, *Order on Application for Waiver of Court Fees and Costs*

You must serve the other parent. If the local child support agency is involved, serve it too.
This means someone 18 or over—not you—must serve the other parent copies of your filed court forms at least **16 court days** before the hearing. Add 5 calendar days if you serve by mail within California (see Code of Civil Procedure section 1005 for other situations). Court days are weekdays when the court is open for business (Monday through Friday except court holidays). **Calendar days** include all days of the month, including weekends and holidays. To determine court and calendar days, go to www.courtinfo.ca.gov/selfhelp/courtcalendars/.

The server must also serve blank copies of these forms:
- FL-320, *Responsive Declaration to Order to Show Cause or Notice of Motion* and FL-150, *Income and Expense Declaration*, or
- FL-155, *Financial Statement (Simplified)*

Then the server fills out and signs a *Proof of Service* (form FL-330 or FL-335). Take this form to the clerk and file it.

Go to your hearing and ask the judge to change the support. Bring your tax returns from the last two years and your last two months' pay stubs. The judge will look at your information, listen to both parents, and make an order. After the hearing, fill out:
- FL-340, *Findings and Order After Hearing* and
- FL-342, *Child Support Information and Order Attachment*

Need help?

Contact the family law facilitator in your county or call your county's bar association and ask for an experienced family lawyer.

FL-192 [Rev. July 1, 2007]

NOTICE OF RIGHTS AND RESPONSIBILITIES
Health-Care Costs and Reimbursement Procedures

Page 2 of 2

8/12

PETITIONER/PLAINTIFF:		CASE NUMBER:
RESPONDENT/DEFENDANT:		ND066521
OTHER PARENT:		

SPOUSAL, PARTNER OR FAMILY SUPPORT ORDER ATTACHMENT

TO ☐ *Findings and Order After Hearing* ☒ *Judgment* ☐ *Other (specify):*

THE COURT FINDS

1. A printout of a computer calculation of the parties' financial circumstances is attached for all required items not filled out below.

2. Net income. The parties' monthly income and deductions are as follows: *(complete a, b, or both):*

	Total gross monthly income	Total monthly deductions	Total hardship deductions	Net monthly disposable income
a. Petitioner: ☐ receiving TANF/CalWORKS				
b. Respondent: ☐ receiving TANF/CalWORKS				

3. Other factors regarding spousal or partner support
   a. ☐ The parties were married for *(specify numbers):* _____ years _____ months.
   b. ☐ The parties were registered as domestic partners or the equivalent on *(date):*
   c. ☐ The Family Code section 4320 factors were considered, as listed in Attachment 3c.
   d. ☐ The marital standard of living was *(describe):*

   ☐ See Attachment 3d.
   e. ☐ Other *(specify):*

THE COURT ORDERS

4. a. The ☐ petitioner ☐ respondent must pay to the ☐ petitioner ☐ respondent
   as ☐ temporary ☐ spousal support ☐ family support ☐ partner support
   $ _____ per month, beginning *(date):* _____ , payable through *(specify end date):* _____

   ☐ payable on the *(specify):* _____ day of each month.
   ☐ Other *(specify):*

   b. ☐ Support must be paid by check, money order, or cash. The support payor's obligation to pay support will terminate on the death, remarriage, or registration of a new domestic partnership of the support payee.

   c. ☐ An earnings assignment for the foregoing support will issue. (Note: The payor of spousal, family, or partner support is responsible for the payment of support directly to the recipient until support payments are deducted from the payor's earnings, and for any support not paid by the assignment.)

   d. ☐ Service of the earnings assignment is stayed provided the payor is not more than *(specify number):* _____ days late in the payment of spousal, family, or partner support.

Page 1 of 2

Form Approved for Optional Use
Judicial Council of California
FL-343 [Rev. January 1, 2005]

SPOUSAL, PARTNER, OR FAMILY SUPPORT ORDER ATTACHMENT
(Family Law)

Family Code, §§ 150, 299, 3651, 3653, 3654, 4320, 4330, 4337

Legal Solutions Plus

5. ☐ The parties must promptly inform each other of any change of employment, including the employer's name, address, and telephone number.

6. ☐ NOTICE: It is the goal of this state that each party must make reasonable good faith efforts to become self-supporting as provided for in Family Code section 4320. The failure to make reasonable good faith efforts may be one of the factors considered by the court as a basis for modifying or terminating support.

7. ☐ This order is for family support. Both parties must complete and file with the court a *Child Support Case Registry Form* (form FL-191) within 10 days of the date of this order. The parents must notify the court of any change of information submitted within 10 days of the change by filing an updated form. Form FL-192, *Notice of Rights and Responsibilities* and *Information Sheet on Changing a Child Support Order*, is attached.

8. ☐ The issue of spousal or partner support for the ☐ petitioner ☐ respondent is reserved for a later determination.

9. ☒ The court terminates jurisdiction over the issue of spousal or partner support for the ☒ petitioner ☒ respondent.

10. ☐ Other (specify):

NOTICE: Any party required to pay support must pay interest on overdue amounts at the "legal" rate, which is currently 10 percent.

THIS IS A COURT ORDER

FL-343 [Rev. January 1, 2004] SPOUSAL, PARTNER, OR FAMILY SUPPORT ORDER ATTACHMENT Page 2 of 2
(Family Law)

10 of 12

PETITIONER:	CASE NUMBER
RESPONDENT:	ND066521

PROPERTY ORDER ATTACHMENT TO JUDGMENT

1. **Division of community property assets**

   a. [X] There are no community property assets.

   b. [ ] The court finds that the net value of the community estate is less than $5,000 and that the [ ] petitioner [ ] respondent cannot be found. Under Family Code section 2604, the entire community estate is awarded to the [ ] petitioner [ ] respondent.

   c. [ ] The petitioner will receive the following assets: *(Attach additional page if necessary.)*

   d. [ ] The respondent will receive the following assets: *(Attach additional page if necessary.)*

   e. The [ ] petitioner [ ] respondent will be responsible for preparing and filing a *Qualified Domestic Relations Order* (QDRO) to divide the following plan or retirement account(s) *(specify):*

   The fee for preparation of the QDRO shall be shared as follows *(specify):*

   f. [ ] Other orders:

   g. [ ] Each spouse will receive the assets listed above as his or her sole and separate property. The parties must execute any and all documents required to carry out this division.

   h. The court reserves jurisdiction to divide any community assets not listed here and enforce the terms of this order.

2. **Division of community property debts**

   a. [X] There are no community debts.

   b. [ ] All community debts have been paid by the [ ] petitioner [ ] respondent.
   The [ ] petitioner [ ] respondent must reimburse the other party: $
   The payment plan is as follows:

   c. [ ] The petitioner will be responsible for the following debts: *(Attach additional page if necessary.)*

   d. [ ] The respondent will be responsible for the following debts: *(Attach additional page if necessary.)*

Form Approved for Optional Use
Judicial Council of California
FL-345 [Rev. January 1, 2007]

PROPERTY ORDER ATTACHMENT TO JUDGMENT
(Family Law)

Legal Solutions Plus

Family Code §§ 299, 2500-2660

11-8-12

46 | Page

PETITIONE		CASE NUMBER.
RESPONDENT:		ND066521

e. ☐ Other orders:

f. Each party will be solely responsible for paying the debts assigned to him or her and will hold the other harmless from those debts. The parties understand that the creditors are not bound by this judgment. If a creditor seeks payment from the party who is not listed as responsible for the debt, that party can file a motion to seek reimbursement from the defaulting party.

g. The court reserves jurisdiction to divide any community debts not listed here.

3. ☐ Equalization of division of property and debt orders. To equalize the division of the community property assets and debts, the ☐ petitioner ☐ respondent must pay to the other the sum of: $, payable as follows (specify):

4. Separate property

a. ☒ The court confirms the following assets or debts as the sole separate property, or sole responsibility, of the petitioner:

Any and all assets and obligations acquired or incurred by Petitioner on or after the date of separation, July 1, 2003.

b. ☒ The court confirms the following assets or debts as the sole separate property, or sole responsibility, of the respondent:

Any and all assets and obligations acquired or incurred by Respondent on or after the date of separation, July 1, 2003.

5. ☐ The settlement agreement between the parties dated (date): is attached and made a part of this judgment.

6. ☐ Sale of property. The following property will be offered for sale and sold for the fair market value as soon as a willing buyer can be found, and the net proceeds from the sale will be ☐ divided equally ☐ other (specify):

7. ☐ Other orders (specify):

PROPERTY ORDER ATTACHMENT TO JUDGMENT
(Family Law)

EXHIBIT '3':
Applicant's Marriage Certificate

COUNTY OF LOS ANGELES
REGISTRAR-RECORDER/COUNTY CLERK

4 2018 19 011211

LICENSE AND CERTIFICATE OF MARRIAGE
MUST BE LEGIBLE - MAKE NO ERASURES, WHITEOUTS OR OTHER ALTERATIONS
USE DARK INK ONLY

STATE FILE NUMBER · LOCAL REGISTRATION NUMBER

1A. FIRST NAME · 1B. MIDDLE

1C. CURRENT LAST

3. DATE OF BIRTH (MM/DD/CCYY) **07/21/1980** · 4. STATE/COUNTRY OF BIRTH **MEX** · 5. # PREV. MARRIAGES/SRDP **1** · 5A. LAST MARRIAGE/SRDP ENDED BY · 5B. DATE ENDED (MM/DD/CCYY) **06/12/2012**

6. ADDRESS · 7. CITY **LONG BEACH** · 8. STATE/COUNTRY **CA** · 9. ZIP CODE **90813**

10B. STATE OF BIRTH (IF OUTSIDE U.S. ENTER COUNTRY) **MEX**

11B. STATE OF BIRTH (IF OUTSIDE U.S. ENTER COUNTRY) **MEX**

12A. FIRST NAME · 12B. MIDDLE

12C. CURRENT LAST · 12D. LAST NAME AT BIRTH (IF DIFFERENT THAN 12C)

13. DATE OF BIRTH (MM/DD/CCYY) **12/17/1983** · 14. STATE/COUNTRY OF BIRTH **MEX** · 15. # PREV. MARRIAGES/SRDP **0** · 16A. LAST MARRIAGE/SRDP ENDED BY · 16B. DATE ENDED (MM/DD/CCYY) **--/--/----**

17. ADDRESS · 18. CITY **LONG BEACH** · 19. STATE/COUNTRY **CA** · 20. ZIP CODE **90813**

21A. FULL BIRTH NAME OF FATHER/PARENT · 21B. STATE OF BIRTH (IF OUTSIDE U.S. ENTER COUNTRY) **MEX**

22B. STATE OF BIRTH (IF OUTSIDE U.S. ENTER COUNTRY) **MEX**

WE, THE UNDERSIGNED DECLARE UNDER PENALTY OF PERJURY UNDER THE LAWS OF THE STATE OF CALIFORNIA THAT WE ARE UNMARRIED AND THAT THE FOREGOING INFORMATION IS TRUE AND CORRECT TO THE BEST OF OUR KNOWLEDGE AND BELIEF. WE FURTHER DECLARE THAT NO LEGAL OBJECTION TO THE MARRIAGE NOR TO THE ISSUANCE OF A LICENSE IS KNOWN TO US. WE ACKNOWLEDGE RECEIPT OF THE INFORMATION REQUIRED BY FAMILY CODE SECTION 358 AND HEREBY APPLY FOR A LICENSE AND CERTIFICATE OF MARRIAGE.

23. SIGNATURE OF PERSON LISTED IN FIELDS 1A-1D · 24. SIGNATURE OF PERSON LISTED IN FIELDS 12A-12D

25A. ISSUE DATE (MM/DD/CCYY) **05/24/2018** · 25B. EXPIRES AFTER (MM/DD/CCYY) **08/22/2018** · 25C. NAME OF COUNTY CLERK **DEAN C. LOGAN** · SIGNATURE OF CLERK OR DEPUTY CLERK

25E. MARRIAGE LICENSE NUMBER **P2532576** · 25F. COUNTY OF ISSUE **LOS ANGELES** · RETURN COMPLETED MARRIAGE LICENSE TO FOLLOWING ADDRESS: **12400 Imperial Highway, Norwalk, CA 90650**

26A. SIGNATURE OF WITNESS · 26B. NAME OF PERSON WITNESSING MARRIAGE (TYPE OR PRINT CLEARLY)

26C. ADDRESS, CITY, STATE/COUNTRY, AND ZIP CODE

27A. SIGNATURE OF WITNESS **Gricelda Acuña** · NAME OF PERSON WITNESSING MARRIAGE (TYPE OR PRINT CLEARLY)

27C. ADDRESS, CITY, STATE/COUNTRY, AND ZIP CODE

28A. DATE OF MARRIAGE (MM/DD/CCYY) **05/29/2018** · 28B. CITY/TOWN OF MARRIAGE **NORWALK** · 28C. COUNTY OF MARRIAGE **LOS ANGELES**

29A. SIGNATURE OF PERSON SOLEMNIZING MARRIAGE · 29B. RELIGIOUS DENOMINATION (IF CLERGY)

29C. NAME OF PERSON SOLEMNIZING MARRIAGE (TYPE OR PRINT CLEARLY) **MARIA URIBE** · 29D. OFFICIAL TITLE **DEPUTY COMMISSIONER**

29E. ADDRESS, CITY, STATE/COUNTRY, AND ZIP CODE **12400 E. IMPERIAL HIGHWAY, NORWALK, CA 90650**

NEW NAME(S) · 30A. FIRST - MUST BE SAME AS 1A **MARIA** · 30B. MIDDLE **ALEJANDRA** · 30C. LAST **HEREDIA RODRIGUEZ**

31A. FIRST - MUST BE SAME AS 12A · 31B. MIDDLE · 31C. LAST

32A. NAME OF LOCAL REGISTRAR **DEAN C. LOGAN** · 32B. SIGNATURE OF CLERK OR DEPUTY CLERK · 32C. DATE ACCEPTED FOR REGISTRATION **MAY 3 0 2016**

STATE OF CALIFORNIA, DEPARTMENT OF PUBLIC HEALTH, OFFICE OF VITAL RECORDS

CAL05ANGC2

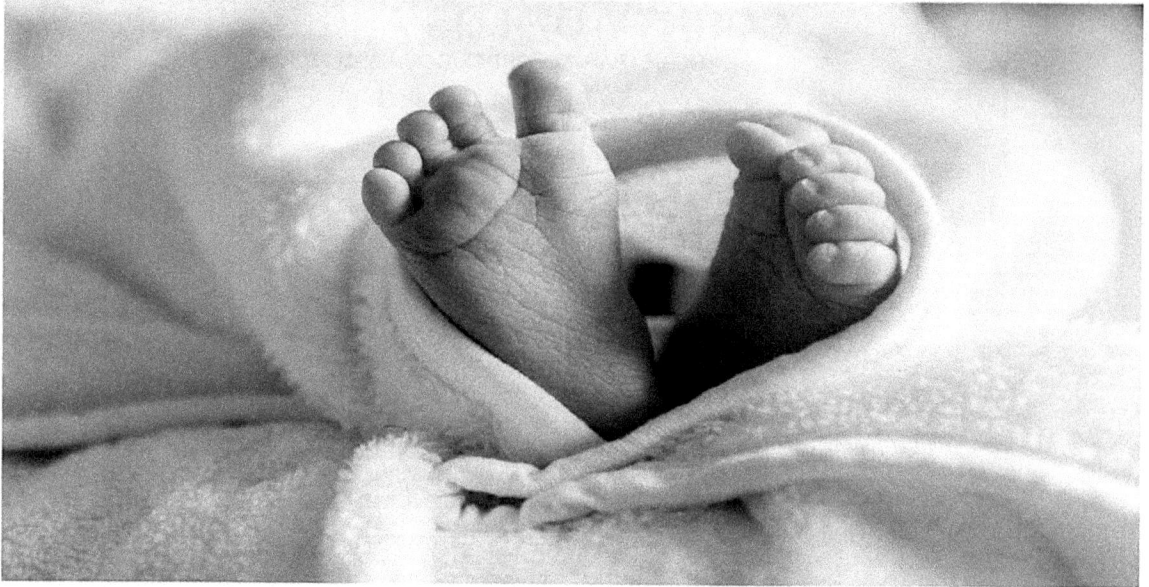

COUNTY OF LOS ANGELES • REGISTRAR-RECORDER/COUNTY CLERK

CERTIFICATE OF LIVE BIRTH
STATE OF CALIFORNIA
USE BLACK INK ONLY

1-1999-62   003331

STATE FILE NUMBER   LOCAL REGISTRATION DISTRICT AND CERTIFICATE NUMBER

THIS CHILD	1A. NAME OF CHILD — FIRST (GIVEN)	1B. MIDDLE	1C. LAST (FAMILY)	
	2. SEX: MALE	3A. THIS BIRTH SINGLE, TWIN, ETC.: SINGLE	3B. IF MULTIPLE, THIS CHILD 1ST, 2ND, ETC.: –	4A. DATE OF BIRTH — MM/DD/CCYY: 05/15/1999	4B. HOUR — (24 HOUR CLOCK TIME): 0911
PLACE OF BIRTH	5A. PLACE OF BIRTH — NAME OF HOSPITAL OR FACILITY: LONG BEACH COMMUNITY MED CTR	5B. STREET ADDRESS — STREET NUMBER OR LOCATION		
	5C. CITY: LONG BEACH	5D. COUNTY: LOS ANGELES	5E. PLANNED PLACE OF BIRTH: HOSPITAL	
FATHER OF CHILD	6A. NAME OF FATHER — FIRST (GIVEN)	6B. MIDDLE: DAVID	6C. LAST (FAMILY)	7. STATE OF BIRTH: CA 8. DATE OF BIRTH: 04/22/1981
MOTHER OF CHILD	10A. MOTHER — FIRST (GIVEN)	10B. MIDDLE: ALEJANDRA	10C. LAST (FAMILY)	11. STATE OF BIRTH: MEXICO 11. DATE OF BIRTH: 07/21/1980

INFORMANT CERTIFICATION	I CERTIFY THAT I HAVE REVIEWED THE STATUS INFORMATION AND THAT IT IS TRUE AND CORRECT TO THE BEST OF MY KNOWLEDGE.	12A. PARENT OR OTHER INFORMANT — SIGNATURE	12B. RELATIONSHIP TO CHILD: FATHER	12C. DATE SIGNED: 05/17/1999
CERTIFICATION OF BIRTH	I CERTIFY THAT THE CHILD WAS BORN ALIVE AT THE DATE, TIME AND PLACE STATED	13A. ATTENDANT CERTIFIER — SIGNATURE — DEGREE OR TITLE	13B. LICENSE NUMBER: A041250	13C. DATE SIGNED: 5/19/99
	13C. TYPED NAME, TITLE AND MAILING ADDRESS OF ATTENDANT: JOHN CARDIN, MD, 1760 TERMINO, LONG BEACH		14. TYPED NAME AND TITLE OF CERTIFIER OTHER THAN ATTENDANT: MICHAEL FONG, MED.REC.DIRECTOR	
LOCAL REGISTRAR	15A. DATE OF DEATH	15B. STATE FILE NO. (STATE USE ONLY)	16. LOCAL REGISTRAR — SIGNATURE	17. DATE ACCEPTED FOR REGISTRATION: 05/20/1999

This is to certify that this document is a true copy of the official record filed with the Registrar-Recorder/County Clerk.

SEP 2 9 2011

DEAN C. LOGAN
Registrar-Recorder/County Clerk

This copy not valid unless prepared on engraved border displaying the Seal and signature of the Registrar-Recorder/County Clerk.

001314130

ANY ALTERATION OR ERASURE VOIDS THIS CERTIFICATE

51 | P a g e

CITY OF LONG BEACH

DEPARTMENT OF HEALTH AND HUMAN SERVICES
LONG BEACH, CALIFORNIA

CERTIFICATE OF LIVE BIRTH 1-2000-62 007158
STATE OF CALIFORNIA
USE BLACK INK ONLY

THIS CHILD	2. SEX: MALE	3A. THIS BIRTH, SINGLE, TWIN, ETC: SINGLE	4A. DATE OF BIRTH: 10/10/2000 — HOUR: 1443
PLACE OF BIRTH	ST. MARY MEDICAL CENTER	1050 LINDEN AVENUE	HOSPITAL
	LONG BEACH	LOS ANGELES	
FATHER OF CHILD			STATE OF BIRTH: CA — DATE OF BIRTH: 04/22/1981
MOTHER OF CHILD			STATE OF BIRTH: MEXICO — DATE OF BIRTH: 07/21/1980

INFORMANT CERTIFICATION — BIRTH CLERK — 10/12/2000

CERTIFICATION OF BIRTH — LICENSE NUMBER A68555 — 10/12/2000

M CHEN, MD, 1050 LINDEN AVENUE, LONG BEACH — B SOHL, MD.

LOCAL REGISTRAR — 10/16/2000

115085

CERTIFIED COPY OF VITAL RECORDS

STATE OF CALIFORNIA } SS   DATE ISSUED OCT 2 6 2000
CITY OF LONG BEACH

This is a true and exact reproduction of the document officially registered and placed on file in the office of the VITAL RECORDS SECTION, LONG BEACH DEPARTMENT OF HEALTH AND HUMAN SERVICES.

DARRYL M. SEXTON, M.D.
CITY HEALTH OFFICER
REGISTRAR OF VITAL RECORDS

This copy not valid unless prepared on engraved border displaying seal and signature of the Registrar

ANY ALTERATION OR ERASURE VOIDS THIS CERTIFICATE

CITY OF LONG BEACH

DEPARTMENT OF HEALTH AND HUMAN SERVICES
LONG BEACH, CALIFORNIA

CERTIFICATE OF LIVE BIRTH
STATE OF CALIFORNIA
USE BLACK INK ONLY

1-2003-62   000250
LOCAL REGISTRATION DISTRICT AND CERTIFICATE NUMBER

STATE FILE NUMBER

THIS CHILD	1A. NAME OF CHILD — FIRST (GIVEN)	1B. MIDDLE		1C. LAST (FAMILY)	
	2. SEX FEMALE	3A. THIS BIRTH SINGLE	3B. IF MULTIPLE, THIS CHILD 1ST, 2ND, ETC.	4A. DATE OF BIRTH — MM/DD/YY 01/11/2003	4B. HOUR 1158

PLACE OF BIRTH

5A. PLACE OF BIRTH — NAME OF HOSPITAL OR FACILITY ST. MARY MEDICAL CENTER	5B. STREET ADDRESS — STREET NUMBER, OR LOCATION 1050 LINDEN AVENUE	
5C. CITY LONG BEACH	5D. COUNTY LOS ANGELES	5E. PLANNED PLACE OF BIRTH HOSPITAL

FATHER OF CHILD

6A. NAME OF FATHER — FIRST (GIVEN)	6B. MIDDLE	6C. LAST (FAMILY)	7. STATE OF BIRTH CA	8. DATE OF BIRTH 04/22/1981

MOTHER OF CHILD

9A. NAME OF MOTHER — FIRST (GIVEN)	9B. MIDDLE	9C. LAST (FAMILY)	10. STATE OF BIRTH MEXICO	11. DATE OF BIRTH 07/21/1980

INFORMANT CERTIFICATION

I CERTIFY THAT I HAVE REVIEWED THE STATED INFORMATION AND THAT IT IS TRUE AND CORRECT TO THE BEST OF MY KNOWLEDGE.

12A. PARENT OR OTHER INFORMANT — SIGNATURE

13A. RELATIONSHIP TO CHILD MOTHER	13B. DATE SIGNED 01/16/2003

CERTIFICATION OF BIRTH

I CERTIFY THAT THE CHILD WAS BORN ALIVE AT THE DATE, HOUR AND PLACE STATED.

13B. LICENSE NUMBER A68965	13C. DATE SIGNED 01/16/2003

13D. TYPED NAME, TITLE AND MAILING ADDRESS OF ATTENDANT
STEPHANIE HANDELMAN, MD, 1050 LINDEN AVENUE, LONG BEACH

14. TYPED NAME AND TITLE OF CERTIFIER IF OTHER THAN ATTENDANT
VIRGINIA BOHR, HIS COORD

LOCAL REGISTRAR

15A. DATE OF DEATH	15B. STATE FILE NO. (DATE USE ONLY)	16. LOCAL REGISTRAR — SIGNATURE	17. DATE ACCEPTED FOR REGISTRATION 01/21/2003

195179

CERTIFIED COPY OF VITAL RECORDS

CITY OF LONG BEACH
DEPARTMENT OF HEALTH AND HUMAN SERVICES
LONG BEACH, CALIFORNIA

CERTIFICATE OF LIVE BIRTH
STATE OF CALIFORNIA
USE BLACK INK ONLY

1201162005609

FEMALE SINGLE	08/17/2011	0820

PLACE OF BIRTH, NAME OF HOSPITAL OR FACILITY
LONG BEACH MEMORIAL MED CTR

LONG BEACH	LOS ANGELES

MARIA	ALEJANDRA	HEREDIA RAMIREZ	MEXICO	07/21/1980

	MOTHER	08/18/2011
	A 033956	08/18/2011

NARENDER BHATIA, MD, 3200 LONG BEACH, LONG BEACH | JOY SARTI, HEALTH IS

HELENE CALVET, MD | 08/23/2011

COUNTY OF LOS ANGELES
REGISTRAR-RECORDER/COUNTY CLERK

CERTIFICATE OF LIVE BIRTH
STATE OF CALIFORNIA
USE BLACK INK ONLY

1201562000771
LOCAL REGISTRATION NUMBER

MALE	SINGLE	02/04/2015	1330

PLACE OF BIRTH: LONG BEACH MEMORIAL MED CTR
LONG BEACH
LOS ANGELES

MARIA | ALEJANDRA | HEREDIA RAMIREZ | MEXICO | 07/21/1980

MOTHER | 02/06/2015
A68667 | 02/06/2015

RABIN MIZRAHI, MD, 1043 ATLANTIC AVE #508, LONG BEACH | JOY SARTI, HEALTH IS

MITCHELL KUSHNER, MD | 02/09/2015

MemorialCare.
Miller Children's & Women's
Hospital Long Beach

Children's Home Society
of California

cert.verification.430639
VERIFICATION LETTER

FEB 04 2020

Health Information Management
Birth Certificate

T 562-933-1146
F 562-933-1185

2801 Atlantic Avenue
Long Beach, California 90806
memorialcare.org

12/29/2019

LONG BEACH MEMORIAL MEDICAL CENTER
2801 ATLANTIC AVE
LONG BEACH CA 90806

OUR MEDICAL RECORDS INDICATE THAT THE FOLLOWING CHILD:

███████████████████

WAS BORN IN THIS FACILITY
ON 12/28/2019 AT 0345 HOURS

BIRTH PARENT'S BIRTH NAME:
████████████████████

BIRTH PARENT'S BIRTH PLACE: JAL, MX   DOB: 07/21/1980

PARENT'S BIRTH NAME:
████████████████

PARENT'S BIRTH PLACE: MICH, MX   DOB: 12/17/1983

SEX OF CHILD: FEMALE

BIRTH ATTENDANT: NARENDER NATH BHATIA, MD

HOSPITAL REPRESENTATIVE

*THIS IS NOT A BIRTH CERTIFICATE

Page 1

SUPERIOR COURT OF CALIFORNIA
COUNTY OF LOS ANGELES

NO. 8DY07564   PAGE NO. 1
THE PEOPLE OF THE STATE OF CALIFORNIA   VS.   CURRENT DATE 09/10/20
DEFENDANT 01: MARIA ALEJANDRA CABRERA
LAW ENFORCEMENT AGENCY EFFECTING ARREST: DOWNEY POLICE DEPARTMENT

BAIL: APPEARANCE   AMOUNT   DATE   RECEIPT OR   SURETY COMPANY   REGISTER
        DATE   OF BAIL   POSTED   BOND NO.   NUMBER

CASE FILED ON 11/10/08.
 COMPLAINT FILED, DECLARED OR SWORN TO CHARGING DEFENDANT WITH HAVING
COMMITTED, ON OR ABOUT 10/17/08 IN THE COUNTY OF LOS ANGELES, THE FOLLOWING
OFFENSE(S) OF:
    COUNT 01: 23152(A) VC MISD
    COUNT 02: 23152(B) VC MISD
    COUNT 03: 14601.1(A) VC MISD
NEXT SCHEDULED EVENT:
 12/24/08   830 AM ARRAIGNMENT   DIST DOWNEY COURTHOUSE DEPT 004

ON 11/14/08 AT 800 AM :

  NOTICE: CONVICTION OF THIS OFFENSE WILL REQUIRE THE DEFENDANT TO
  PROVIDE DNA SAMPLES AND PRINT IMPRESSIONS PURSUANT TO PENAL CODE
  SECTIONS 296 AND 296.1 IF THE DEFENDANT HAS SUFFERED A PRIOR
  FELONY CONVICTION. WILLFUL REFUSAL TO PROVIDE THE SAMPLES AND
  IMPRESSIONS IS A CRIME.
  NOTICE: THE PEOPLE OF THE STATE OF CALIFORNIA INTEND TO PRESENT
  EVIDENCE AND SEEK JURY FINDINGS REGARDING ALL APPLICABLE
  CIRCUMSTANCES IN AGGRAVATION, PURSUANT TO PENAL CODE SECTION
  1170(B) AND CUNNINGHAM V. CALIFORNIA 2007 U.S. LEXIS 1324.

ON 12/24/08 AT 830 AM IN DOWNEY COURTHOUSE DEPT 004

CASE CALLED FOR ARRAIGNMENT
PARTIES: DEBRA COLE-HALL (JUDGE) NANCY COVARRUBIAS (CLERK)
         YOLANDA HUFF (REP)   SONJA S. MIN (DA)
DEFENDANT IS PRESENT IN COURT, AND NOT REPRESENTED BY COUNSEL

  DEFENDANT APPEARS IN PRO PER
DEFENDANT PERSONALLY WAIVES RIGHT TO COUNSEL, APPEARING IN PROPRIA PERSONA.
 COURT ADVISES DEFENDANT THAT SELF-REPRESENTATION IS ALMOST ALWAYS AN UNWISE
  CHOICE, AND WILL NOT WORK TO HIS ADVANTAGE; FURTHER, THAT HE WILL NOT BE
  HELPED OR TREATED WITH SPECIAL LENIENCY BY THE COURT OR THE PROSECUTOR, AND
  THAT HE WILL BE HELD TO THE SAME STANDARDS OF CONDUCT AS AN ATTORNEY.
  FURTHER, IF HE WISHES TO REPRESENT HIMSELF, HE WILL NOT BE ABLE TO CLAIM
  LATER THAT HE MADE A MISTAKE, OR THAT HE RECEIVED INEFFECTIVE ASSISTANCE OF
  COUNSEL.
 COURT FINDS THAT THE DEFENDANT VOLUNTARILY AND INTELLIGENTLY CHOOSES
  SELF-REPRESENTATION, AND THAT HE KNOWINGLY, INTELLIGENTLY, UNDERSTANDINGLY,
  AND EXPLICITLY WAIVES HIS RIGHT TO COUNSEL, AND DETERMINES THAT DEFENDANT IS
  COMPETENT TO REPRESENT HIMSELF.
DEFENDANT WAIVES FURTHER ARRAIGNMENT.
DEFENDANT ADVISED OF AND PERSONALLY AND EXPLICITLY WAIVES THE FOLLOWING RIGHTS:

WRITTEN ADVISEMENT OF RIGHTS AND WAIVERS FILED, INCORPORATED BY REFERENCE HEREIN
  REPRESENTATION BY COUNSEL;
TRIAL BY COURT AND TRIAL BY JURY
  CONFRONTATION AND CROSS-EXAMINATION OF WITNESSES;
  SUBPOENA OF WITNESSES INTO COURT TO TESTIFY IN YOUR DEFENSE;
  AGAINST SELF-INCRIMINATION;
DEFENDANT ADVISED OF THE FOLLOWING:
  THE NATURE OF THE CHARGES AGAINST HIM, THE ELEMENTS OF THE OFFENSE IN THE
  COMPLAINT, AND POSSIBLE DEFENSES TO SUCH CHARGES;
THE POSSIBLE CONSEQUENCES OF A PLEA OF GUILTY OR NOLO CONTENDERE, INCLUDING
  THE MAXIMUM PENALTY AND ADMINISTRATIVE SANCTIONS AND THE POSSIBLE LEGAL
  EFFECTS AND MAXIMUM PENALTIES INCIDENT TO SUBSEQUENT CONVICTIONS FOR THE
  SAME OR SIMILAR OFFENSES;
THE EFFECTS OF PROBATION;
IF YOU ARE NOT A CITIZEN, YOU ARE HEREBY ADVISED THAT A CONVICTION OF THE
  OFFENSE FOR WHICH YOU HAVE BEEN CHARGED WILL HAVE THE CONSEQUENCES OF
  DEPORTATION, EXCLUSION FROM ADMISSION TO THE UNITED STATES, OR DENIAL OF

  NATURALIZATION PURSUANT TO THE LAWS OF THE UNITED STATES.
COURT FINDS THAT EACH SUCH WAIVER IS KNOWINGLY, UNDERSTANDINGLY, AND EXPLICITLY
  MADE;
THE DEFENDANT WITH THE COURTS APPROVAL, PLEADS NOLO CONTENDERE TO COUNT 02 A
  VIOLATION OF SECTION 23152(B) VC. THE COURT FINDS THE DEFENDANT GUILTY.
COUNT (02) : DISPOSITION: CONVICTED
  COURT ORDERS AND FINDINGS:
  -TAHL WAIVER IS ORDERED FILED.
COURT FINDS THAT THERE IS A FACTUAL BASIS FOR DEFENDANT'S PLEA, AND COURT
  ACCEPTS PLEA.
WAIVES TIME FOR SENTENCE.
NEXT SCHEDULED EVENT:
  SENTENCING
  DEFENDANT WAIVES ARRAIGNMENT FOR JUDGMENT AND STATES THERE IS NO LEGAL CAUSE
WHY SENTENCE SHOULD NOT BE PRONOUNCED. THE COURT ORDERED THE FOLLOWING
JUDGMENT:
AS TO COUNT (02):
IMPOSITION OF SENTENCE SUSPENDED
DEFENDANT PLACED ON SUMMARY PROBATION
  FOR A PERIOD OF 036 MONTHS UNDER THE FOLLOWING TERMS AND CONDITIONS:
  PAY A FINE OF $390.00

  OR SERVE 13 DAYS IN LOS ANGELES COUNTY JAIL LESS CREDIT FOR 1 DAYS
  TOTAL: 12 DAYS
    PLUS A STATE PENALTY FUND ASSESSMENT OF $864.00
  PLUS $1.00 NIGHT COURT.
  PLUS $72.00 CRIMINAL FINE SURCHARGE (PURSUANT TO 1465.7 P.C.)
    $20.00 COURT SECURITY ASSESSMENT (PURSUANT TO 1465.8(A)(1) P.C.)
    $35.00 INSTALLMENT & ACCOUNTS RECEIVABLE FEE (PURSUANT TO 1205(D)PC)
    $10.00 CITATION PROCESSING FEE (PURSUANT TO 1463.07 P.C.)
    $50.00 ALCOHOL ABUSE/PREVENTION ASSESSMENT (23645 V.C.)
    $33.00 LABORATORY SERVICE FUND(PURSUANT TO 1463.14(B) P.C.)
  DEFENDANT TO PAY FINE TO THE COURT CLERK
THE DEFENDANT SHALL ENROLL AND PARTICIPATE IN AND SUCCESSFULLY COMPLETE, A
3-MONTH LICENSED FIRST-OFFENDER ALCOHOL AND OTHER DRUG EDUCATION AND COUNSELING
  PROGRAM
  DEFENDANT SHALL PAY A RESTITUTION FINE IN THE AMOUNT OF $100.00 TO THE COURT

TOTAL DUE: $1,545.00
IN ADDITION:
-ENROLL WITHIN 21 DAYS IN AN AB-541 PROGRAM.
-DO NOT DRIVE ANY VEHICLE WITH ANY MEASURABLE AMOUNT OF ALCOHOL
 OR DRUGS IN YOUR BLOOD OR REFUSE TO TAKE AND COMPLETE ANY BLOOD
 ALCOHOL OR DRUG CHEMICAL TEST, ANY FIELD SOBRIETY TEST, AND ANY
 PRELIMINARY ALCOHOL SCREENING TEST, WHEN REQUESTED BY ANY PEACE
 OFFICER.
-DO NOT DRIVE A MOTOR VEHICLE WITHOUT A VALID DRIVER'S LICENSE IN
 YOUR POSSESSION OR WITHOUT LIABILITY INSURANCE IN AT LEAST THE
 MINIMUM AMOUNTS REQUIRED BY LAW.
-OBEY ALL LAWS AND ORDERS OF THE COURT.
-DEFENDANT ACKNOWLEDGES TO THE COURT THAT THE DEFENDANT
 UNDERSTANDS AND ACCEPTS ALL THE PROBATION CONDITIONS, AND
 DEFENDANT AGREES TO ABIDE BY SAME.
-THE COURT ORDERS THE DEFENDANT TO APPEAR ON THE NEXT COURT DATE.
COURT ORDERS AND FINDINGS:
-THE DEFENDANT WAS ADVISED AND UNDERSTOOD THAT BEING UNDER THE

   INFLUENCE OF ALCOHOL OR DRUGS, OR BOTH, IMPAIRS HIS/HER ABILITY
   TO SAFELY OPERATE A MOTOR VEHICLE, AND IT IS EXTREMELY DANGEROUS
   TO HUMAN LIFE TO DRIVE WHILE UNDER THE INFLUENCE OF ALCOHOL OR
   DRUGS, OR BOTH. DEFENDANT WAS FURTHER ADVISED THAT IF HE/SHE
   CONTINUES TO DRIVE WHILE UNDER THE INFLUENCE OF ALCOHOL OR
   DRUGS, OR BOTH, AND AS A RESULT OF HIS/HER DRIVING, SOMEONE IS
   KILLED, THE DEFENDANT CAN BE CHARGED WITH MURDER.
MATTER IS CONTINUED FOR PROOF OF ENROLLMENT IN AB541
TO 01-26-09 AT 8:30 AM IN DEPT. 5.

$1545.00 IS DUE BY 12-24-09.
COUNT (02): DISPOSITION: CONVICTED
REMAINING COUNTS DISMISSED:
   COUNT (01): DISMISSED DUE TO PLEA NEGOTIATION
   COUNT (03): DISMISSED DUE TO PLEA NEGOTIATION
ABSTRACT ISSUED ON 12/24/08 FOR COUNT 02
DMV JUDGMENT CODE QWG
NEXT SCHEDULED EVENT:
  01/26/09   830 AM PROOF OF ENROLLMENT   DIST DOWNEY COURTHOUSE DEPT 004
NEXT SCHEDULED EVENT:
  12/24/09   900 AM FINES/FEES   DIST DOWNEY COURTHOUSE DEPT CLK

CUSTODY STATUS: ON PROBATION

12/24/08 ARREST DISPOSITION REPORT SENT VIA FILE TRANSFER TO DEPARTMENT OF
          JUSTICE. LAST DISPOSITION DATE: 12/24/08.

ON 01/26/09 AT 830 AM IN DOWNEY COURTHOUSE DEPT 004

CASE CALLED FOR PROOF OF ENROLLMENT
PARTIES: DEBRA COLE-HALL (JUDGE) NANCY COVARRUBIAS (CLERK)
                 ANTHONETTE DEAR   (REP) SONJA S. MIN (DA)
DEFENDANT IS PRESENT IN COURT, AND NOT REPRESENTED BY COUNSEL
  DEFENDANT APPEARS IN PRO PER
  PROOF OF ENROLLMENT IN AB541 IS RECEIVED AND FILED.
  DEFENDANT TO FILE COMPLETION OF AB541 IN CLERK'S OFFICE
  BY 4-27-09.
  ($1545.00 REMAINS DUE ON 12-24-09).
  COURT ORDERS AND FINDINGS:
  -OTHER TERMS AND CONDITIONS OF PROBATION TO REMAIN IN FULL FORCE

AND EFFECT.
-THE COURT ORDERS THE DEFENDANT TO APPEAR ON THE NEXT COURT DATE.
NEXT SCHEDULED EVENT:
04/27/09 900 AM PROOF OF DUI SCHOOL DIST DOWNEY COURTHOUSE DEPT CLK

CUSTODY STATUS: ON PROBATION

ON 05/05/09 AT 900 AM IN DOWNEY COURTHOUSE DEPT CLK

CASE CALLED FOR PROOF OF COMPLETION
PARTIES: NONE (JUDGE) NONE (CLERK)
              NONE   (REP) NONE (DDA)
DEFENDANT IS NOT PRESENT IN COURT, AND NOT REPRESENTED BY COUNSEL
   THE DEFENDANT HAS FILED PROOF OF COMPLETION OF AB541.
NEXT SCHEDULED EVENT:
FINES/FEES

ON 12/24/09 AT 900 AM IN DOWNEY COURTHOUSE DEPT CLK

CASE CALLED FOR FINES/FEES
PARTIES: NONE (JUDGE) NONE (CLERK)
              NONE   (REP) NONE (DDA)
DEFENDANT IS PRESENT IN COURT, AND NOT REPRESENTED BY COUNSEL
   OWN RECOGNIZANCE RELEASE SIGNED AND FILED. DEFENDANT GIVEN 60
DAY EXTENSION TO PAY FINE.
   TB
NEXT SCHEDULED EVENT:
   02/24/10 900 AM FINES/FEES DIST DOWNEY COURTHOUSE DEPT CLK

ON 03/03/10 AT 830 AM IN DOWNEY COURTHOUSE DEPT 004

CASE CALLED FOR FINES/FEES
PARTIES: DEBRA COLE-HALL (JUDGE) MARYANNE LAPINTA (CLERK)
              LOUISE COSTELLO   (REP) MICHELE D GILMER (DA)

DEFENDANT IS PRESENT IN COURT, AND NOT REPRESENTED BY COUNSEL
   DEFENDANT APPEARS IN PRO PER
   COURT ORDERS AND FINDINGS:
   -THE COURT ORDERS THE DEFENDANT TO APPEAR ON THE NEXT COURT DATE.
NEXT SCHEDULED EVENT:
   08/03/10 900 AM FINES/FEES DIST DOWNEY COURTHOUSE DEPT CLK

CUSTODY STATUS: ON PROBATION

ON 08/10/10 AT 830 AM IN DOWNEY COURTHOUSE DEPT CLK

CASE CALLED FOR FINES/FEES
PARTIES: NONE (JUDGE) NONE (CLERK)
              NONE   (REP) NONE (DDA)
DEFENDANT IS PRESENT IN COURT, AND NOT REPRESENTED BY COUNSEL
   DEFENDANT APPEARS IN PRO PER
   PAYMENT IN THE AMOUNT OF $200.00 PAID ON 08/10/10 RECEIPT # DOW458653005
NEXT SCHEDULED EVENT:

CASE NO. 8DY07564   PAGE NO.   5
DEF NO. 01   DATE PRINTED 09/10/20

FINES/FEES

ON 08/10/10 AT 900 AM :

   OWN RECOGNIZANCE SIGNED AND FILE.   DEFENDANT WAS GIVEN A
   6 MONTH EXTENSION TO PAY THE FINE.
   BB
NEXT SCHEDULED EVENT:
   02/03/11   830 AM FINES/FEES   DIST DOWNEY COURTHOUSE DEPT 004

ON 10/21/10 AT 900 AM IN DOWNEY COURTHOUSE DEPT CLK

CASE CALLED FOR FINES/FEES
PARTIES: NONE (JUDGE) NONE (CLERK)

            NONE   (REP) NONE (DDA)
DEFENDANT IS NOT PRESENT IN COURT, AND NOT REPRESENTED BY COUNSEL
PAYMENT IN THE AMOUNT OF $150.00 PAID ON 10/21/10 RECEIPT # DOW514964011
NEXT SCHEDULED EVENT:
FINES/FEES

ON 02/03/11 AT 830 AM IN DOWNEY COURTHOUSE DEPT 004

CASE CALLED FOR FINES/FEES
PARTIES: DEBRA COLE-HALL (JUDGE) MARYANNE LAPINTA   (CLERK)
              LA TASHA M. PETERS (REP)   SARAH D. SLICE (DA)
THE DEFENDANT FAILS TO APPEAR, WITHOUT SUFFICIENT EXCUSE AND NOT REPRESENTED BY
   COUNSEL
   PROBATION REVOKED
AS TO COUNT (02):
DMV ABSTRACT NOT REQUIRED
NEXT SCHEDULED EVENT:
   BENCH/WARRANT TO ISSUE

02/03/11 BENCH WARRANT IN THE AMOUNT OF $36,000.00 BY ORDER OF JUDGE DEBRA
   COLE-HALL ISSUED. (02/03/11).

ON 02/18/11 AT 830 AM IN DOWNEY COURTHOUSE DEPT CLK

CASE CALLED FOR FINES/FEES
PARTIES: NONE (JUDGE) NONE (CLERK)
              NONE   (REP) NONE (DDA)
DEFENDANT IS PRESENT IN COURT, AND NOT REPRESENTED BY COUNSEL
   DEFENDANT APPEARS IN PRO PER
PAYMENT IN THE AMOUNT OF $1,000.00 PAID ON 02/18/11 RECEIPT # DOW290934007
NEXT SCHEDULED EVENT:
FINES/FEES

ON 02/18/11 AT 830 AM IN DOWNEY COURTHOUSE DEPT 004

CASE CALLED FOR BENCH WARRANT HEARING

PARTIES: DEBRA COLE-HALL (JUDGE) MARYANNE LAPINTA   (CLERK)
            LOUISE COSTELLO (REP)   NONE (DA)
DEFENDANT IS PRESENT IN COURT, AND NOT REPRESENTED BY COUNSEL
   DEFENDANT APPEARS IN PRO PER
PROBATION REINSTATED
   PROBATION IS CONTINUED ON THE SAME TERMS AND CONDITIONS WITH THE FOLLOWING
      MODIFICATIONS:
AS TO COUNT (02):
   DEFENDANT TO PAY $1000.00 TODAY AND BALANCE BY 4-18-11
DMV ABSTRACT NOT REQUIRED
NEXT SCHEDULED EVENT:
   02/18/11   900 AM FINES/FEES   DIST DOWNEY COURTHOUSE DEPT CLK
NEXT SCHEDULED EVENT:
   04/18/11   900 AM FINES/FEES   DIST DOWNEY COURTHOUSE DEPT CLK

CUSTODY STATUS: ON PROBATION

ON 02/18/11 AT 900 AM IN DOWNEY COURTHOUSE DEPT CLK

CASE CALLED FOR FINES/FEES
PARTIES: NONE (JUDGE) NONE (CLERK)
            NONE   (REP) NONE (DDA)
DEFENDANT IS PRESENT IN COURT, AND NOT REPRESENTED BY COUNSEL
   DEFENDANT APPEARS IN PRO PER
PAYMENT IN THE AMOUNT OF $100.00 PAID ON 02/18/11 RECEIPT # DOW290934009
NEXT SCHEDULED EVENT:
FINES/FEES

02/18/11 BENCH WARRANT IN THE AMOUNT OF $36,000.00   RECALLED. (02/18/11).

ON 04/20/11 AT 830 AM IN DOWNEY COURTHOUSE DEPT 004

CASE CALLED FOR COURT CONSIDERATION
PARTIES: DEBRA COLE-HALL (JUDGE) NONE (CLERK)
            NONE (REP)   NONE ()
DEFENDANT IS NOT PRESENT IN COURT, AND NOT REPRESENTED BY COUNSEL

   PROBATION REVOKED
AS TO COUNT (02):
   IN CHAMBERS: THE DEFENDANT FAILED TO PAY FINE BALANCE $95.00
   BY 4-18-11.
DMV ABSTRACT NOT REQUIRED
NEXT SCHEDULED EVENT:
   BENCH/WARRANT TO ISSUE

04/22/11 BENCH WARRANT IN THE AMOUNT OF $46,000.00 BY ORDER OF JUDGE DEBRA
   COLE-HALL ISSUED. (04/28/11).

ON 05/05/11 AT 830 AM IN DOWNEY COURTHOUSE DEPT 004

CASE CALLED FOR BENCH WARRANT HEARING
PARTIES: DEBRA COLE-HALL (JUDGE) GINA M. BLACK   (CLERK)
            LOUISE COSTELLO (REP)   GREGORY R. MOHRMAN (DA)
DEFENDANT IS PRESENT IN COURT, AND NOT REPRESENTED BY COUNSEL
PROBATION REINSTATED

CASE NO. 8DY07564   PAGE NO.   7
DEF NO. 01   DATE PRINTED 09/10/20

   PROBATION IS CONTINUED ON THE SAME TERMS AND CONDITIONS WITH THE FOLLOWING
      MODIFICATIONS:
AS TO COUNT (02):
   DEFENDANT TO PAY FINE FORTHWITH.
DMV ABSTRACT NOT REQUIRED
NEXT SCHEDULED EVENT:
   PROCEEDINGS TERMINATED

ON 05/05/11 AT 900 AM IN DOWNEY COURTHOUSE DEPT CLK

CASE CALLED FOR FINES/FEES
PARTIES: NONE (JUDGE) NONE (CLERK)
             NONE   (REP) NONE (DDA)
DEFENDANT IS PRESENT IN COURT, AND NOT REPRESENTED BY COUNSEL
   DEFENDANT APPEARS IN PRO PER
PAYMENT IN THE AMOUNT OF $95.00 PAID ON 05/05/11 RECEIPT # DOW257520005

NEXT SCHEDULED EVENT:
PROCEEDINGS TERMINATED

05/05/11 BENCH WARRANT IN THE AMOUNT OF $46,000.00   RECALLED. (05/05/11).

09/10/20

I HEREBY CERTIFY THIS TO BE A TRUE AND CORRECT COPY OF THE ELECTRONIC DOCKET
ON FILE IN THIS OFFICE AS OF THE ABOVE DATE.
SHERRI R. CARTER ,EXECUTIVE OFFICER/CLERK OF SUPERIOR COURT, COUNTY OF LOS
ANGELES, STATE OF CALIFORNIA

BY _____, DEPUTY

EXHIBIT '6':
Applicant's 2018 Federal Income Tax Return

Form 1040 Department of the Treasury—Internal Revenue Service (99)
U.S. Individual Income Tax Return **2018** OMB No. 1545-0074 IRS Use Only—Do not write or staple in this space.

Filing status: ☐ Single ☐ Married filing jointly ☐ Married filing separately ☒ Head of household ☐ Qualifying widow(er)

Your first name and initial	Last name		Your social security number
████	████		████

Your standard deduction: ☐ Someone can claim you as a dependent ☐ You were born before January 2, 1954 ☐ You are blind

If joint return, spouse's first name and initial	Last name		Spouse's social security number

Spouse standard deduction: ☐ Someone can claim your spouse as a dependent ☐ Spouse was born before January 2, 1954 ☒ Full-year health care coverage or exempt (see inst.)
☐ Spouse is blind ☐ Spouse itemizes on a separate return or you were dual-status alien

Home address (number and street). If you have a P.O. box, see instructions.
████ | Apt. no. | Presidential Election Campaign (see inst.) ☐ You ☐ Spouse

City, town or post office, state, and ZIP code. If you have a foreign address, attach Schedule 6.
LONG BEACH CA 90813 | If more than four dependents, see inst. and ✓ here ▶ ☐

Dependents (see instructions):

(1) First name Last name	(2) Social security number	(3) Relationship to you	(4) ✓ if qualifies for (see inst.): Child tax credit / Credit for other dependents
████	████	██	☒ ☐
████████████	████████	████	☒ ☐
			☐ ☐
			☐ ☐

Sign Here

Under penalties of perjury, I declare that I have examined this return and accompanying schedules and statements, and to the best of my knowledge and belief, they are true, correct, and complete. Declaration of preparer (other than taxpayer) is based on all information of which preparer has any knowledge.

Joint return?
See instructions.
Keep a copy for your records.

Your signature	Date	Your occupation INSURANCE BROKER	If the IRS sent you an Identity Protection PIN, enter it here (see inst.)
Spouse's signature. If a joint return, both must sign.	Date	Spouse's occupation	If the IRS sent you an Identity Protection PIN, enter it here (see inst.)

Paid Preparer Use Only

Preparer's name MARIA A CABRERA	Preparer's signature	PTIN P01627109	Firm's EIN 46-1474677	Check if: ☐ 3rd Party Designee
Firm's name ▶ DESTINY INSURANCE		Phone no. 562-987-1810		☐ Self-employed
Firm's address ▶ 356 REDONDO AVE LONG BEACH CA 90802-				

For Disclosure, Privacy Act, and Paperwork Reduction Act Notice, see separate instructions. Form **1040** (2018)
BCA

	1	Wages, salaries, tips, etc. Attach Form(s) W-2				1	
Attach Form(s) W-2. Also attach Form(s) W-2G and 1099-R if tax was withheld.	2a	Tax-exempt interest	2a		b Taxable interest	2b	
	3a	Qualified dividends . .	3a		b Ordinary dividends	3b	
	4a	IRAs, pensions, and annuities	4a		b Taxable amount	4b	
	5a	Social security benefits	5a		b Taxable amount	5b	
	6	Total income. Add lines 1 through 5. Add any amount from Schedule 1, line 22 18,631				6	18,631
Standard Deduction for—	7	Adjusted gross income. If you have no adjustments to income, enter the amount from line 6; otherwise, subtract Schedule 1, line 36, from line 6				7	17,314
• Single or married filing separately, $12,000	8	Standard deduction or itemized deductions (from Schedule A)				8	18,000
• Married filing jointly or Qualifying widow(er), $24,000	9	Qualified business income deduction (see instructions)				9	0
• Head of household, $18,000	10	Taxable income. Subtract lines 8 and 9 from line 7. If zero or less, enter -0-				10	0
• If you checked any box under Standard deduction, see instructions	11	a Tax (see inst) _____ (check if any from: 1 ☐ Form(s) 8814 2 ☐ Form 4972 3 ☐ _____)					
		b Add any amount from Schedule 2 and check here . . . . ▶ ☐				11	
	12	a Child tax credit/credit for other dependents _____ b Add any amount from Schedule 3 and check here ▶ ☐				12	
	13	Subtract line 12 from line 11. If zero or less, enter -0-				13	
	14	Other taxes. Attach Schedule 4				14	2,633
	15	Total tax. Add lines 13 and 14				15	2,633
	16	Federal income tax withheld from Forms W-2 and 1099				16	
	17	Refundable credits: a EIC (see inst.) _5,716_ b Sch 8812 _2,222_ c Form 8863 _____					
		Add any amount from Schedule 5 _____				17	7,938
	18	Add lines 16 and 17. These are your total payments				18	7,938
Refund	19	If line 18 is more than line 15, subtract line 15 from line 18. This is the amount you overpaid				19	5,305
Direct deposit? See instructions.	20a	Amount of line 19 you want refunded to you. If Form 8888 is attached, check here . . . ▶ ☐				20a	5,305
▶ b		Routing number ███████ ▶ c Type: ☒ Checking ☐ Savings					
▶ d		Account number					
	21	Amount of line 19 you want applied to your 2019 estimated tax . . . ▶	21				
Amount You Owe	22	Amount you owe. Subtract line 18 from line 15. For details on how to pay, see instructions . . . . . ▶				22	
	23	Estimated tax penalty (see instructions) . . . . ▶	23				

Go to www.irs.gov/Form1040 for instructions and the latest information.   Form **1040** (2018)

SCHEDULE 1
(Form 1040)

Department of the Treasury
Internal Revenue Service

Additional Income and Adjustments to Income

▶ Attach to Form 1040.
▶ Go to *www.irs.gov/Form1040* for instructions and the latest information.

OMB No. 1545-0074

2018

Attachment
Sequence No. **01**

Name(s) shown on Form 1040

Your social security number

Additional Income	1–9b	Reserved	1–9b	
	10	Taxable refunds, credits, or offsets of state and local income taxes	10	
	11	Alimony received	11	
	12	Business income or (loss). Attach Schedule C or C-EZ	12	18,631
	13	Capital gain or (loss). Attach Schedule D if required. If not required, check here ▶ ☐	13	
	14	Other gains or (losses). Attach Form 4797	14	
	15a	Reserved	15b	
	16a	Reserved	16b	
	17	Rental real estate, royalties, partnerships, S corporations, trusts, etc. Attach Schedule E	17	
	18	Farm income or (loss). Attach Schedule F	18	
	19	Unemployment compensation	19	
	20a	Reserved	20b	
	21	Other income. List type and amount ▶	21	
	22	Combine the amounts in the far right column. If you don't have any adjustments to income, enter here and include on Form 1040, line 6. Otherwise, go to line 23	22	18,631

Adjustments to Income	23	Educator expenses	23		
	24	Certain business expenses of reservists, performing artists, and fee-basis government officials. Attach Form 2106	24		
	25	Health savings account deduction. Attach Form 8889	25		
	26	Moving expenses for members of the Armed Forces. Attach Form 3903	26		
	27	Deductible part of self-employment tax. Attach Schedule SE	27	1,317	
	28	Self-employed SEP, SIMPLE, and qualified plans	28		
	29	Self-employed health insurance deduction	29		
	30	Penalty on early withdrawal of savings	30		
	31a	Alimony paid b Recipient's SSN ▶	31a		
	32	IRA deduction	32		
	33	Student loan interest deduction	33		
	34	Tuition and fees. Attach Form 8917	34		
	35	Reserved	35		
	36	Add lines 23 through 35	36		1,317

For Paperwork Reduction Act Notice, see your tax return instructions.

Schedule 1 (Form 1040) 2018

BCA

SCHEDULE 4
(Form 1040)

Department of the Treasury
Internal Revenue Service

Other Taxes

▶ Attach to Form 1040.
▶ Go to *www.irs.gov/Form1040* for instructions and the latest information.

OMB No. 1545-0074

2018

Attachment
Sequence No. 04

Name(s) shown on Form 1040

Your social security number

Other Taxes	57	Self-employment tax. Attach Schedule SE	57	2,633
	58	Unreported social security and Medicare tax from: Form a ☐ 4137 b ☐ 8919	58	
	59	Additional tax on IRAs, other qualified retirement plans, and other tax-favored accounts. Attach Form 5329 if required	59	
	60a	Household employment taxes. Attach Schedule H	60a	
	b	Repayment of first-time homebuyer credit from Form 5405. Attach Form 5405 if required	60b	
	61	Health care: individual responsibility (see instructions)	61	
	62	Taxes from: a ☐ Form 8959 b ☐ Form 8960		
		c ☐ Instructions; enter code(s) _____	62	
	63	Section 965 net tax liability installment from Form 965-A 63		
	64	Add the amounts in the far right column. These are your **total other taxes.** Enter here and on Form 1040, line 14	64	2,633

For Paperwork Reduction Act Notice, see your tax return instructions.

Schedule 4 (Form 1040) 2018

BCA

SCHEDULE 6
(Form 1040)

Department of the Treasury
Internal Revenue Service

Foreign Address and Third Party Designee

► Attach to Form 1040.
► Go to *www.irs.gov/Form1040* for instructions and the latest information.

OMB No. 1545-0074

2018

Attachment
Sequence No. **05A**

Name(s) shown on Form 1040			Your social security number
██████████████████			████████████████

Foreign Address	Foreign country name	Foreign province/county	Foreign postal code

Third Party Designee	Do you want to allow another person to discuss this return with the IRS (see instructions)?		☒ **Yes. Complete below.** ☐ No
	Designee's name ► ████████████	Phone	Personal identification number (PIN) ► 11111

For Paperwork Reduction Act Notice, see your tax return instructions.

Schedule 6 (Form 1040) 2018

BCA

SCHEDULE C
(Form 1040)

Department of the Treasury
Internal Revenue Service (99)

Profit or Loss From Business
(Sole Proprietorship)

► Go to *www.irs.gov/ScheduleC* for instructions and the latest information.
► Attach to Form 1040, 1040NR, or 1041; partnerships generally must file Form 1065.

OMB No. 1545-0074

2018

Attachment
Sequence No. **09**

Name of proprietor	Social security number (SSN)

A	Principal business or profession, including product or service (see instructions)	B Enter code from instructions
	DESTINY INSURANCE	► 524210
C	Business name. If no separate business name, leave blank.	D Employer ID number (EIN) (see instr.)

E	Business address (including suite or room no.) ►
	City, town or post office, state, and ZIP code

F	Accounting method:	(1) [X] Cash	(2) [ ] Accrual	(3) [ ] Other (specify) ►		
G	Did you "materially participate" in the operation of this business during 2018? If "No," see instructions for limit on losses				[X] Yes	[ ] No
H	If you started or acquired this business during 2018, check here			►		
I	Did you make any payments in 2018 that would require you to file Form(s) 1099? (see instructions)				[ ] Yes	[X] No
J	If "Yes," did you or will you file required Forms 1099?				[ ] Yes	[ ] No

Part I — Income

1	Gross receipts or sales. See instructions for line 1 and check the box if this income was reported to you on Form W-2 and the "Statutory employee" box on that form was checked ► [ ]	1	47,271
2	Returns and allowances	2	
3	Subtract line 2 from line 1	3	47,271
4	Cost of goods sold (from line 42)	4	
5	Gross profit. Subtract line 4 from line 3	5	47,271
6	Other income, including federal and state gasoline or fuel tax credit or refund (see instructions)	6	
7	Gross income. Add lines 5 and 6 ►	7	47,271

Part II — Expenses. Enter expenses for business use of your home only on line 30.

8	Advertising	8	500	18	Office expense (see instructions)	18	
9	Car and truck expenses (see instructions)	9		19	Pension and profit-sharing plans	19	
				20	Rent or lease (see instructions):		
10	Commissions and fees	10		a	Vehicles, machinery, and equipment	20a	
11	Contract labor (see instructions)	11		b	Other business property	20b	19,800
12	Depletion	12		21	Repairs and maintenance	21	
13	Depreciation and section 179 expense deduction (not included in Part III) (see instructions)	13		22	Supplies (not included in Part III)	22	2,500
				23	Taxes and licenses	23	4,583
				24	Travel and meals:		
14	Employee benefit programs (other than on line 19)	14		a	Travel	24a	
15	Insurance (other than health)	15	1,257	b	Deductible meals (see instructions)	24b	
16	Interest (see instructions):			25	Utilities	25	
a	Mortgage (paid to banks, etc.)	16a		26	Wages (less employment credits)	26	
b	Other	16b		27a	Other expenses (from line 48)	27a	
17	Legal and professional services	17		b	Reserved for future use	27b	

28	Total expenses before expenses for business use of home. Add lines 8 through 27a ►	28	28,640
29	Tentative profit or (loss). Subtract line 28 from line 7	29	18,631
30	Expenses for business use of your home. Do not report these expenses elsewhere. Attach Form 8829 unless using the simplified method (see instructions). Simplified method filers only: enter the total square footage of: (a) your home _____ and (b) the part of your home used for business: _____. Use the Simplified Method Worksheet in the instructions to figure the amount to enter on line 30.	30	
31	Net profit or (loss). Subtract line 30 from line 29. • If a profit, enter on both Schedule 1 (Form 1040), line 12 (or Form 1040NR, line 13) and on Schedule SE, line 2. (If you checked the box on line 1, see instructions) Estates and trusts, enter on Form 1041, line 3. • If a loss, you must go to line 32.	31	18,631
32	If you have a loss, check the box that describes your investment in this activity (see instructions). • If you checked 32a, enter the loss on both Schedule 1 (Form 1040), line 12 (or Form 1040NR, line 13) and on Schedule SE, line 2. (If you checked the box on line 1, see the line 31 instructions). Estates and trusts, enter on Form 1041, line 3. • If you checked 32b, you must attach Form 6198. Your loss may be limited.	32a [ ] All investment is at risk. 32b [ ] Some investment is not at risk.	

For Paperwork Reduction Act Notice, see the separate Instructions.
BCA

Schedule C (Form 1040) 2018

Earned Income Credit

Qualifying Child Information

▶ Complete and attach to Form 1040 only if you have a qualifying child.
▶ Go to www.irs.gov/ScheduleEIC for the latest information.

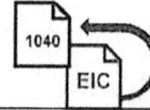

1040

EIC

OMB No. 1545-0074

2018

Attachment
Sequence No. 43

Name(s) shown on return

Your social security number

Before you begin:
- See the instructions for Form 1040, line 17a, to make sure that (a) you can take the EIC, and (b) you have a qualifying child.
- Be sure the child's name on line 1 and social security number (SSN) on line 2 agree with the child's social security card. Otherwise, at the time we process your return, we may reduce or disallow your EIC. If the name or SSN on the child's social security card is not correct, call the Social Security Administration at 1-800-772-1213.

⚠ CAUTION
- You can't claim the EIC for a child who didn't live with you for more than half of the year.
- If you take the EIC even though you are not eligible, you may not be allowed to take the credit for up to 10 years. See the instructions for details.
- It will take us longer to process your return and issue your refund if you do not fill in all lines that apply for each qualifying child.

Qualifying Child Information

		Child 1		Child 2		Child 3	
		First name	Last name	First name	Last name	First name	Last name
1	**Child's name** If you have more than three qualifying children, you have to list only three to get the maximum credit.	███		███			
2	**Child's SSN** The child must have an SSN as defined in the instructions for Form 1040, line 17a, unless the child was born and died in 2018. If your child was born and died in 2018 and did not have an SSN, enter "Died" on this line and attach a copy of the child's birth certificate, death certificate, or hospital medical records showing a live birth.	███		███			
3	**Child's year of birth**	Year 2015 If born after 1999 and the child is younger than you (or your spouse, if filing jointly), skip lines 4a and 4b; go to line 5.		Year 2011 If born after 1999 and the child is younger than you (or your spouse, if filing jointly), skip lines 4a and 4b; go to line 5.		Year ____ If born after 1999 and the child is younger than you (or your spouse, if filing jointly), skip lines 4a and 4b; go to line 5.	
4 a	Was the child under age 24 at the end of 2018, a student, and younger than you (or your spouse, if filing jointly)?	☐ Yes. Go to line 5.	☐ No. Go to line 4b.	☐ Yes. Go to line 5.	☐ No. Go to line 4b.	☐ Yes. Go to line 5.	☐ No. Go to line 4b.
b	Was the child permanently and totally disabled during any part of 2018?	☐ Yes. Go to line 5.	☐ No. The child is not a qualifying child.	☐ Yes. Go to line 5.	☐ No. The child is not a qualifying child.	☐ Yes. Go to line 5.	☐ No. The child is not a qualifying child.
5	**Child's relationship to you** (for example, son, daughter, grandchild, niece, nephew, eligible foster child, etc.)	SON		DAUGHTER			
6	**Number of months child lived with you in the United States during 2018** • If the child lived with you for more than half of 2018 but less than 7 months, enter "7." • If the child was born or died in 2018 and your home was the child's home for more than half the time he or she was alive during 2018, enter "12."	12 months Do not enter more than 12 months.		12 months Do not enter more than 12 months.		____ months Do not enter more than 12 months.	

For Paperwork Reduction Act Notice, see your tax return instructions.
BCA

Schedule EIC (Form 1040) 2018

Name of person with self-employment income (as shown on Form 1040 or Form 1040NR)	Social security number of person with self-employment income ▶

Section B—Long Schedule SE

Part I Self-Employment Tax

Note: If your only income subject to self-employment tax is **church employee income**, see instructions. Also see instructions for the definition of church employee income.

A	If you are a minister, member of a religious order, or Christian Science practitioner and you filed Form 4361, but you had $400 or more of **other** net earnings from self-employment, check here and continue with Part I . . . . . . ▶ ☐			
1 a	Net farm profit or (loss) from Schedule F, line 34, and farm partnerships, Schedule K-1 (Form 1065), box 14, code A. **Note:** Skip lines 1a and 1b if you use the farm optional method (see instructions) .	1a		
b	If you received social security retirement or disability benefits, enter the amount of Conservation Reserve Program payments included on Schedule F, line 4b, or listed on Schedule K-1 (Form 1065), box 20, code AH	1b	(	)
2	Net profit or (loss) from Schedule C, line 31; Schedule C-EZ, line 3; Schedule K-1 (Form 1065), box 14, code A (other than farming); and Schedule K-1 (Form 1065-B), box 9, code J1. Ministers and members of religious orders, see instructions for types of income to report on this line. See instructions for other income to report. **Note:** Skip this line if you use the nonfarm optional method (see instructions)	2	18,631	
3	Combine lines 1a, 1b, and 2	3	18,631	
4 a	If line 3 is more than zero, multiply line 3 by 92.35% (0.9235). Otherwise, enter amount from line 3	4a	17,206	
	Note: If line 4a is less than $400 due to Conservation Reserve Program payments on line 1b, see instructions.			
b	If you elect one or both of the optional methods, enter the total of lines 15 and 17 here	4b		
c	Combine lines 4a and 4b. If less than $400, **stop**; you don't owe self-employment tax. **Exception:** If less than $400 and you had **church employee income**, enter -0- and continue ▶	4c	17,206	
5 a	Enter your **church employee income** from Form W-2. See instructions for definition of church employee income 5a			
b	Multiply line 5a by 92.35% (0.9235). If less than $100, enter -0-	5b		
6	Add lines 4c and 5b	6	17,206	
7	Maximum amount of combined wages and self-employment earnings subject to social security tax or the 6.2% portion of the 7.65% railroad retirement (tier 1) tax for 2018	7	128,400	00
8 a	Total social security wages and tips (total of boxes 3 and 7 on Form(s) W-2) and railroad retirement (tier 1) compensation. If $128,400 or more, skip lines 8b through 10, and go to line 11 . . . . 8a			
b	Unreported tips subject to social security tax (from Form 4137, line 10) 8b			
c	Wages subject to social security tax (from Form 8919, line 10) . . . 8c			
d	Add lines 8a, 8b, and 8c	8d		
9	Subtract line 8d from line 7. If zero or less, enter -0- here and on line 10 and go to line 11 ▶	9	128,400	
10	Multiply the smaller of line 6 or line 9 by 12.4% (0.124)	10	2,134	
11	Multiply line 6 by 2.9% (0.029)	11	499	
12	Self-employment tax. Add lines 10 and 11. Enter here and on **Schedule 4 (Form 1040), line 57,** or Form 1040NR, line 55	12	2,633	
13	Deduction for one-half of self-employment tax. Multiply line 12 by 50% (0.50). Enter the result here and on **Schedule 1 (Form 1040), line 27,** or Form 1040NR, line 27 13	1,317		

Part II Optional Methods To Figure Net Earnings (see instructions)

Farm Optional Method. You may use this method only if **(a)** your gross farm income[1] wasn't more than $7,920, **or (b)** your net farm profits[2] were less than $5,717.

14	Maximum income for optional methods	14	5,280	00
15	Enter the **smaller** of: two-thirds (⅔) of gross farm income[1] (not less than zero) **or** $5,280. Also include this amount on line 4b above	15		

Nonfarm Optional Method. You may use this method only if **(a)** your net nonfarm profits[3] were less than $5,717 and also less than 72.189% of your gross nonfarm income,[4] **and (b)** you had net earnings from self-employment of at least $400 in 2 of the prior 3 years. **Caution:** You may use this method no more than five times.

16	Subtract line 15 from line 14	16		
17	Enter the **smaller** of: two-thirds (⅔) of gross nonfarm income[4] (not less than zero) **or** the amount on line 16. Also include this amount on line 4b above	17		

[1] From Sch. F, line 9, and Sch. K-1 (Form 1065), box 14, code B

[2] From Sch. F, line 34, and Sch. K-1 (Form 1065), box 14, code A—minus the amount you would have entered on line 1b had you not used the optional method.

[3] From Sch. C, line 31; Sch. C-EZ, line 3; Sch. K-1 (Form 1065), box 14, code A; and Sch. K-1 (Form 1065-B), box 9, code J1.

[4] From Sch. C, line 7; Sch. C-EZ, line 1; Sch. K-1 (Form 1065), box 14, code C; and Sch. K-1 (Form 1065-B), box 9, code J2.

SCHEDULE 8812
(Form 1040)

Department of the Treasury
Internal Revenue Service (99)

Additional Child Tax Credit

▶Attach to Form 1040 or Form 1040NR.

▶ Go to *www.irs.gov/Schedule8812* for instructions and the latest information.

OMB No. 1545-0074

2018

Attachment
Sequence No. 47

Name(s) shown on return

Your social security number

Part I	All Filers

Caution: If you file Form 2555 or 2555-EZ, **stop here**; you cannot claim the additional child tax credit.

1	If you are required to use the worksheet in Pub. 972, enter the amount from line 10 of the Child Tax Credit and Credit for Other Dependents Worksheet in the publication. Otherwise:			
	1040 filers: Enter the amount from line 8 of your Child Tax Credit and Credit for Other Dependents Worksheet (see the instructions for Form 1040, line 12a).		1	4,000
	1040NR filers: Enter the amount from line 8 of your Child Tax Credit and Credit for Other Dependents Worksheet (see the instructions for Form 1040NR, line 49).			
2	Enter the amount from Form 1040, line 12a, or Form 1040NR, line 49		2	
3	Subtract line 2 from line 1. If zero, stop here; you cannot claim this credit		3	4,000
4	Number of qualifying children under 17 with the required social security number: __2__ X $1,400. Enter the result. If zero, stop here; you cannot claim this credit		4	2,800
	TIP: The number of children you use for this line is the same as the number of children you used for line 1 of the Child Tax Credit and Credit for Other Dependents Worksheet.			
5	Enter the smaller of line 3 or line 4		5	2,800
6 a	Earned income (see separate instructions)	6a 17,314		
b	Nontaxable combat pay (see separate instructions)	6b		
7	Is the amount on line 6a more than $2,500?			
	☐ **No.** Leave line 7 blank and enter -0- on line 8			
	☒ **Yes.** Subtract $2,500 from the amount on line 6a. Enter the result . . .	7 14,814		
8	Multiply the amount on line 7 by 15% (0.15) and enter the result		8	2,222
	Next. On line 4, is the amount $4,200 or more?			
	☒ **No.** If line 8 is zero, stop here; you cannot claim this credit. Otherwise, skip Part II and enter the smaller of line 5 or line 8 on line 15.			
	☐ **Yes.** If line 8 is equal to or more than line 5, skip Part II and enter the amount from line 5 on line 15. Otherwise, go to line 9.			

Part II	Certain Filers Who Have Three or More Qualifying Children

9	Withheld social security, Medicare, and Additional Medicare taxes from Form(s) W-2, boxes 4 and 6. If married filing jointly, include your spouse's amounts with yours. If your employer withheld or you paid Additional Medicare Tax or tier 1 RRTA taxes, see separate instructions	9		
10	**1040 filers:** Enter the total of the amounts from Schedule 1 (Form 1040), line 27, and Schedule 4 (Form 1040), line 58, plus any taxes that you identified using code "UT" and entered on Schedule 4 (Form 1040), line 62.	10		
	1040NR filers: Enter the total of the amounts from Form 1040NR, lines 27 and 56, plus any taxes that you identified using code "UT" and entered on line 60.			
11	Add lines 9 and 10	11		
12	**1040 filers:** Enter the total of the amounts from Form 1040, line 17a, and Schedule 5 (Form 1040), line 72.	12		
	1040NR filers: Enter the amount from Form 1040NR, line 67.			
13	Subtract line 12 from line 11. If zero or less, enter -0-		13	
14	Enter the larger of line 8 or line 13		14	
	Next, enter the smaller of line 5 or line 14 on line 15			

Part III	Additional Child Tax Credit

15	This is your additional child tax credit		15	2,222

Enter this amount on Form 1040, line 17b, or Form 1040NR, line 64.

1040

1040NR ◀ . . . .

For Paperwork Reduction Act Notice, see your tax return instructions.
BCA

Schedule 8812 (Form 1040) 2018

Form **8867**

Department of the Treasury
Internal Revenue Service

Paid Preparer's Due Diligence Checklist

Earned Income Credit (EIC), American Opportunity Tax Credit (AOTC), Child Tax Credit (CTC) (including the Additional Child Tax Credit (ACTC) and Credit for Other Dependents (ODC)), and Head of Household (HOH) Filing Status

▶ To be completed by preparer and filed with Form 1040, 1040NR, 1040SS, or 1040PR.
▶ Go to *www.irs.gov/Form8867* for instructions and the latest information.

OMB No. 1545-0074

2018

Attachment
Sequence No. **70**

Taxpayer name(s) shown on return

Taxpayer identification number

| **Part I** | Due Diligence Requirements |

		EIC	CTC/ ACTC/ODC	AOTC	HOH
	Please check the appropriate box for the credit(s) and/or HOH filing status claimed on this return and complete the related Parts I–V for the benefit(s), and/or HOH filing status claimed (check all that apply).	[X]	[X]	[ ]	[X]

1	Did you complete the return based on information for tax year 2018 provided by the taxpayer or reasonably obtained by you?	[X] Yes	[ ] No	
2	If credits are claimed on the return, did you complete the applicable EIC and/ or CTC/ACTC/ODC worksheets found in the Form 1040, 1040SS, 1040PR, or 1040NR instructions, and/or the AOTC worksheet found in the Form 8863 instructions, or your own worksheet(s) that provides the same information, and all related forms and schedules for each credit claimed?	[X] Yes	[ ] No	[ ] N/A
3	Did you satisfy the knowledge requirement? To meet the knowledge requirement, you must do both of the following ● Interview the taxpayer, ask questions, and document the taxpayer's responses to determine that the taxpayer is eligible to claim the credit(s) and/or HOH filing status. ● Review information to determine that the taxpayer is eligible to claim the credit(s) and/or HOH filing status and the amount of any credit(s) claimed.	[X] Yes	[ ] No	
4	Did any information provided by the taxpayer or a third party for use in preparing the return, or information reasonably known to you, appear to be incorrect, incomplete, or inconsistent? (If "Yes," answer questions 4a and 4b. If "No," go to question 5.)	[ ] Yes	[X] No	
a	Did you make reasonable inquiries to determine the correct, complete, and consistent information?	[ ] Yes	[ ] No	
b	Did you document your inquiries? (Documentation should include the questions you asked, whom you asked, when you asked, the information that was provided, and the impact the information had on your preparation of the return.)	[ ] Yes	[ ] No	
5	Did you satisfy the record retention requirement? To meet the record retention requirement, you must keep a copy of your documentation referenced in 4b, a copy of this Form 8867, a copy of any applicable worksheet(s), a record of how, when, and from whom the information used to prepare Form 8867 and any applicable worksheet(s) was obtained, and a copy of any document(s) provided by the taxpayer that you relied on to determine eligibility for the credit(s) and/or HOH filing status or to compute the amount of the credit(s)	[X] Yes	[ ] No	
	List those documents, if any, that you relied on			
6	Did you ask the taxpayer whether he/she could provide documentation to substantiate eligibility for the credit(s) and/or HOH filing status and the amount of any credit(s) claimed on the return if his/her return is selected for audit?	[X] Yes	[ ] No	
7	Did you ask the taxpayer if any of these credits were disallowed or reduced in a previous year? (If credits were disallowed or reduced, go to question 7a; if not, go to question 8.)	[X] Yes	[ ] No	[ ] N/A
a	Did you complete the required recertification Form 8862?	[ ] Yes	[ ] No	[ ] N/A
8	If the taxpayer is reporting self-employment income, did you ask questions to prepare a complete and correct Form 1040, Schedule C?	[X] Yes	[ ] No	[ ] N/A

For Paperwork Reduction Act Notice, see separate instructions.

BCA

Form **8867** (2018)

Part II	Due Diligence Questions for Returns Claiming EIC (If the return does not claim EIC, go to Part III.)	EIC	CTC/ACTC/ODC	AOTC	HOH
9 a	Have you determined that this taxpayer is, in fact, eligible to claim the EIC for the number of children for whom the EIC is claimed, or to claim the EIC if the taxpayer has no qualifying child? (Skip 9b and 9c if the taxpayer is claiming the EIC and does not have a qualifying child.)	☒ Yes ☐ No			
b	Did you ask the taxpayer if the child lived with the taxpayer for over half of the year, even if the taxpayer has supported the child the entire year? . .	☒ Yes ☐ No			
c	Did you explain to the taxpayer the rules about claiming the EIC when a child is the qualifying child of more than one person (tiebreaker rules)?	☒ Yes ☐ No ☐ N/A			

Part III	Due Diligence Questions for Returns Claiming CTC/ACTC/ODC (If the return does not claim CTC, ACTC, or ODC, go to Part IV.)	EIC	CTC/ACTC/ODC	AOTC	HOH
10	Have you determined that each qualifying person for the CTC/ACTC/ODC is the taxpayer's dependent who is a citizen, national, or resident of the United States		☒ Yes ☐ No		
11	Did you explain to the taxpayer that he/she may not claim the CTC/ACTC if the taxpayer has not lived with the child for over half of the year, even if the taxpayer has supported the child, unless the child's custodial parent has released a claim to exemption for the child?		☒ Yes ☐ No ☐ N/A		
12	Did you explain to the taxpayer the rules about claiming the CTC/ACTC/ODC for a child of divorced or separated parents (or parents who live apart), including any requirement to attach a Form 8332 or similar statement to the return?		☒ Yes ☐ No ☐ N/A		

Part IV	Due Diligence Questions for Returns Claiming AOTC (If the return does not claim AOTC, go to Part V.)	EIC	CTC/ACTC/ODC	AOTC	HOH
13	Did the taxpayer provide the required substantiation for the credit, including a Form 1098-T and/or receipts for the qualified tuition and related expenses for the claimed AOTC?			☐ Yes ☐ No	

Part V	Due Diligence Questions for Claiming HOH (If the return does not claim HOH filing status, go to Part VI.)	EIC	CTC/ACTC/ODC	AOTC	HOH
14	Have you determined that the taxpayer was unmarried or considered unmarried on the last day of the tax year and provided more than half of the cost of keeping up a home for the year for a qualifying person?				☒ Yes ☐ No

Part VI   Eligibility Certification

▶ **You will have complied with all due diligence requirements for claiming the applicable credit(s) and/or HOH filing status on the return of the taxpayer identified above if you:**

A. Interview the taxpayer, ask adequate questions, document the taxpayer's responses on the return or in your notes, review adequate information to determine if the taxpayer is eligible to claim the credit(s) and/or HOH filing status and to determine the amount of the credit(s) claimed;

B. Complete this Form 8867 truthfully and accurately and complete the actions described in this checklist for any applicable credit(s) claimed and HOH filing status, if claimed;

C. Submit Form 8867 in the manner required; and

D. Keep all five of the following records for 3 years from the latest of the dates specified in the Form 8867 instructions under *Document Retention*.

　1. A copy of Form 8867;

　2. The applicable worksheet(s) or your own worksheet(s) for any credit(s) claimed;

　3. Copies of any documents provided by the taxpayer on which you relied to determine eligibility for the credit(s) and/or HOH filing status;

　4. A record of how, when, and from whom the information used to prepare this form and the applicable worksheet(s) was obtained; and

　5. A record of any additional questions you may have asked to determine eligibility to claim the credit(s), and/or HOH filing status and the amount(s) of any credit(s) claimed and the taxpayer's answers.

▶ **If you have not complied with all due diligence requirements, you may have to pay a $520 penalty for each failure to comply related to a claim of an applicable credit or HOH filing status.**

15	Do you certify that all of the answers on this Form 8867 are, to the best of your knowledge, true, correct, and complete?	☒ Yes	☐ No

Form **8867** (2018)

Form **8965**

Department of the Treasury
Internal Revenue Service

Health Coverage Exemptions

▶ Attach to Form 1040.
▶ Go to *www.irs.gov/Form8965* for instructions and the latest information.

OMB No. 1545-0074

2018

Attachment
Sequence No. **75**

Name as shown on return

Your social security number

Complete this form if you have a Marketplace-granted coverage exemption or you are claiming a coverage exemption on your return.

Part I — Marketplace-Granted Coverage Exemptions for Individuals. If you and/or a member of your tax household have an exemption granted by the Marketplace, complete Part I.

	(a) Name of Individual	(b) SSN	(c) Exemption Certificate Number
1			
2			
3			
4			
5			
6			

Part II — Coverage Exemptions Claimed on Your Return for Your Household

7 If you are claiming a coverage exemption because your household income or gross income is below the filing threshold, check here . . . . ▶ ☒

Part III — Coverage Exemptions Claimed on Your Return for Individuals. If you and/or a member of your tax household are claiming an exemption on your return, complete Part III.

	(a) Name of Individual	(b) SSN	(c) Exemption Type	(d) Full Year	(e) Jan	(f) Feb	(g) Mar	(h) Apr	(i) May	(j) June	(k) July	(l) Aug	(m) Sept	(n) Oct	(o) Nov	(p) Dec
8																
9																
10																
11																
12																
13																

For Privacy Act and Paperwork Reduction Act Notice, see your tax return instructions.

Form **8965** (2018)

BCA

2018 **California Resident Income Tax Return**

FORM

540

APE

ATTACH FEDERAL RETURN

18 PBA 524210

A
R
RP

If your California filing status is different from your federal filing status, check the box here . . . . ☐

1 ☐ Single

4 [X] Head of household (with qualifying person). See instructions.

2 ☐ Married/RDP filing jointly. See inst.

5 ☐ Qualifying widow(er). Enter year spouse/RDP died

See instructions.

3 ☐ Married/RDP filing separately. Enter spouse's/RDP's SSN or ITIN above and full name here

6 If someone can claim you (or your spouse/RDP) as a dependent, check the box here. See inst. . . . . 6 ☐

For line 7, line 8, line 9, and line 10: Multiply the amount you enter in the box by the pre-printed dollar amount for that line. **Whole dollars only**

7 **Personal:** If you checked box 1, 3, or 4 above, enter 1 in the box. If you checked box 2 or 5, enter 2, in the box. If you checked the box on line 6, see instructions . . 7 [1] X $118 = $ 118

8 **Blind:** If you (or your spouse/RDP) are visually impaired, enter 1, if both are visually impaired, enter 2 . . . . 8 ☐ X $118 = $

9 **Senior:** If you (or your spouse/RDP) are 65 or older, enter 1; if both are 65 or older, enter 2 . . . . 9 ☐ X $118 = $

10 **Dependents:** Do not include yourself or your spouse/RDP.

	Dependent 1	Dependent 2	Dependent 3
First Name			
Last Name			
SSN			
Dependent's relationship to you	SON	DAUGHTER	

Total dependent exemptions . . . . 10 [2] X $367 = $ 734

11 **Exemption amount:** Add line 7 through line 10. Transfer this amount to line 32 . . . . 11 $ 852

Your name: ███████████████ Your SSN or ITIN: ███████████████

12	State wages from your Form(s) W-2, box 16. 12		. 00
13	Enter federal adjusted gross income from Form 1040, line 7 13	17,314	00
14	California adjustments – subtractions. Enter the amount from Schedule CA (540), line 37, column B . . 14		00
15	Subtract line 14 from line 13. If less than zero, enter the result in parentheses. See instructions 15	17,314	00
16	California adjustments – additions. Enter the amount from Schedule CA (540), line 37, column C 16		00
17	California adjusted gross income. Combine line 15 and line 16 17	17,314	00

18 Enter the larger of   Your California **itemized deductions** from Schedule CA (540), Part II, line 30; **OR**
Your California **standard deduction** shown below for your filing status:
Single or Married/RDP filing separately $4,401
Married/RDP filing jointly, Head of household, or Qualifying widow(er) . . $8,802
If Married/RDP filing separately or the box on line 6 is checked, STOP. See instructions 18   8,802 . 00

19	Subtract line 18 from line 17. This is your **taxable income.** If less than zero, enter -0- 19	8,512	00

31	Tax. Check the box if from: [X] Tax Table [ ] Tax Rate Schedule [ ] FTB 3800 [ ] FTB 3803 31	85	00
32	Exemption credits. Enter the amount from line 11. If your federal AGI is more than $194,504, see instructions 32	852	00
33	Subtract line 32 from line 31. If less than zero, enter -0- 33	0	00
34	Tax. See instructions. Check the box if from: [ ] Schedule G-1 [ ] FTB 5870A 34		00
35	Add line 33 and line 34 35		00

40	Nonrefundable Child and Dependent Care Expenses Credit. See instructions 40		00
43	Enter credit name _____ code ____ and amount 43		00
44	Enter credit name _____ code ____ and amount 44		00
45	To claim more than two credits, see instructions. Attach Schedule P (540) 45		00
46	Nonrefundable renter's credit. See instructions 46		00
47	Add line 40 through line 46. These are your total credits 47		00
48	Subtract line 47 from line 35. If less than zero, enter -0- 48		00

61	Alternative minimum tax. Attach Schedule P (540) 61		00
62	Mental Health Services Tax. See instructions. 62		00
63	Other taxes and credit recapture. See instructions. 63		00
64	Add line 48, line 61, line 62, and line 63. This is your total tax 64		00

71	California income tax withheld. See instructions	71	. 00
72	2018 CA estimated tax and other payments. See instructions	72	. 00
73	Withholding (Form 592-B and/or 593). See instructions	73	. 00
74	Excess SDI (or VPDI) withheld. See instructions	74	. 00
75	Earned Income Tax Credit (EITC)	75	. 00
76	Add lines 71 through 75. These are your total payments. See instructions	76	. 00

91 Use Tax. Do not leave blank. See instructions .... **91** ⬚ 00

If line 91 is zero, check if: [X] No use tax is owed.

☐ You paid your use tax obligation directly to CDTFA.

92	Payments balance. If line 76 is more than line 91, subtract line 91 from line 76	92	. 00
93	Use Tax balance. If line 91 is more than line 76, subtract line 76 from line 91	93	. 00
94	Overpaid tax. If line 92 is more than line 64, subtract line 64 from line 92	94	. 00
95	Amount of line 94 you want applied to your 2019 estimated tax	95	. 00
96	Overpaid tax available this year. Subtract line 95 from line 94	96	. 00
97	Tax due. If line 92 is less than line 64, subtract line 92 from line 64	97	. 00

	Code	Amount
California Seniors Special Fund. See instructions	400	. 00
Alzheimer's Disease and Related Dementia Voluntary Tax Contribution Fund	401	. 00
Rare and Endangered Species Preservation Voluntary Tax Contribution Program	403	. 00

	Code	Amount
California Breast Cancer Research Voluntary Tax Contribution Fund	405	__ 00
California Firefighters' Memorial Fund	406	__ 00
Emergency Food for Families Voluntary Tax Contribution Fund	407	__ 00
California Peace Officer Memorial Foundation Fund	408	__ 00
California Sea Otter Fund	410	__ 00
California Cancer Research Voluntary Tax Contribution Fund	413	__ 00
School Supplies for Homeless Children Fund	422	__ 00
State Parks Protection Fund/Parks Pass Purchase	423	__ 00
Protect Our Coast and Oceans Voluntary Tax Contribution Fund	424	__ 00
Keep Arts in Schools Voluntary Tax Contribution Fund	425	__ 00
State Children's Trust Fund for the Prevention of Child Abuse	430	__ 00
Prevention of Animal Homelessness and Cruelty Fund	431	__ 00
Revive the Salton Sea Fund	432	__ 00
California Domestic Violence Victims Fund	433	__ 00
Special Olympics Fund	434	__ 00
Type 1 Diabetes Research Fund	435	__ 00
California YMCA Youth and Government Voluntary Tax Contribution Fund	436	__ 00
Habitat for Humanity Voluntary Tax Contribution Fund	437	__ 00
California Senior Citizen Advocacy Voluntary Tax Contribution Fund	438	__ 00
Native California Wildlife Rehabilitation Voluntary Tax Contribution Fund	439	__ 00
Rape Backlog Kit Voluntary Tax Contribution Fund	440	__ 00
Organ and Tissue Donor Registry Voluntary Tax Contribution Fund	441	__ 00
National Alliance on Mental Illness California Voluntary Tax Contribution Fund	442	__ 00
Schools Not Prisons Voluntary Tax Contribution Fund	443	__ 00
110 Add code 400 through code 443. This is your total contribution	110	__ 00

Your name: [REDACTED] Your SSN or ITIN: [REDACTED]

111 AMOUNT YOU OWE. If you do not have an amount on line 96, add line 93, line 97, and line 110. See instructions. **Do not send cash.**
Mail to: **FRANCHISE TAX BOARD**
PO BOX 942867
SACRAMENTO CA 94267-0001 . . . . **111** [ ] . 00
Pay online – Go to ftb.ca.gov/pay for more information.

112 Interest, late return penalties, and late payment penalties . . . . **112** [ ] . 00

113 Underpayment of estimated tax. Check the box: ☐ FTB 5805 attached ☐ FTB 5805F attached **113** [ ] . 00

114 Total amount due. See instructions. Enclose, but **do not** staple, any payment . . . . **114** [ ] . 00

115 REFUND OR NO AMOUNT DUE. Subtract the sum of line 110, line 112 and line 113 from line 96. See instructions.
Mail to: **FRANCHISE TAX BOARD**
PO BOX 942840
SACRAMENTO CA 94240-0001 . . . . **115** [ ] . 00

Fill in the information to authorize direct deposit of your refund into one or two accounts. **Do not attach a voided check or a deposit slip.** See instructions.
Have you verified the routing and account numbers? Use whole dollars only.
All or the following amount of my refund (line 115) is authorized for direct deposit into the account shown below:

Routing number	Type	Account number	116 Direct deposit amount
[ ]	☐ Checking ☐ Savings	[ ]	[ ] . 00

The remaining amount of my refund (line 115) is authorized for direct deposit into the account shown below:

Routing number	Type	Account number	117 Direct deposit amount
[ ]	☐ Checking ☐ Savings	[ ]	[ ] . 00

IMPORTANT: See the instructions to find out if you should attach a copy of your complete federal tax return.

To learn about your privacy rights, how we may use your information, and the consequences for not providing the requested information, go to ftb.ca.gov/forms and search for 1131. To request this notice by mail, call 800.852.5711. Under penalties of perjury, I declare that I have examined this tax return, including accompanying schedules and statements, and to the best of my knowledge and belief, it is true, correct, and complete.

Your signature
X

Date

Spouse's/RDP's signature (if a joint tax return, both must sign)
X

Sign Here

It is unlawful to forge a spouse's/RDP's signature.

Joint tax return? (See instructions.)

Your email address. Enter only one email address.

Preferred phone number
[REDACTED]

Paid preparer's signature (declaration of preparer is based on all information of which preparer has any knowledge)

Firm's name (or yours, if self-employed)
[REDACTED]

PTIN
P01627109

Firm's address
[REDACTED]

Firm's FEIN
46-1474677

Do you want to allow another person to discuss this tax return with us? See instructions . . . . . . ☒ Yes ☐ No

Print Third Party Designee's Name
[REDACTED]

Telephone Number
[REDACTED]

098 3105184 Form 540 2018 **Side 5**

2018 Head of Household Filing Status Schedule

CALIFORNIA FORM

3532

Attach to your California Form 540, Long or Short Form 540NR, or Form 540 2EZ.

Name(s) as shown on tax return	SSN or ITIN
▮▮▮▮▮▮▮▮	▮▮▮▮▮▮▮

Part I – Marital Status

1 Check one box below to identify your marital status. See instructions.

a   Not legally married/RDP during 2018 . . . . **1a** [X]

b   Widow/widower (my spouse/RDP died before 01/01/2018) . . . . **1b** [ ]

c   Marriage/RDP was annulled . . . . **1c** [ ]

d   Received final decree of divorce, legal separation, dissolution, or termination of marriage/RDP by 12/31/2018 . . . . **1d** [ ]

e   Legally married/RDP and did not live with spouse/RDP during 2018 . . . . **1e** [ ]

f   Legally married/RDP and lived with spouse/RDP during 2018. List the beginning and ending dates for each period when you
lived together . . . . **1f** [ ]

From: [   ]   To: [   ]   From: [   ]   To: [   ]

Part II – Qualifying Person

2 Check one box below to identify the relationship of the person that qualifies you for the head of household filing status. See instructions.

a   Son, daughter, stepson, or stepdaughter . . . . **2a** [X]

b   Grandchild, brother, sister, half brother, half sister, stepbrother, stepsister, nephew, or niece . . . . **2b** [ ]

c   Eligible foster child . . . . **2c** [ ]

d   Father, mother, stepfather, or stepmother . . . . **2d** [ ]

e   Grandfather, grandmother, son-in-law, daughter-in-law, father-in-law, mother-in-law, brother-in-law,
sister-in-law, uncle, or aunt . . . . **2e** [ ]

Part III – Qualifying Person Information

3 Information about your qualifying person. See instructions.

First Name . . . . ▮▮▮▮▮

Last Name . . . . ▮▮▮▮

SSN . . . . ▮▮▮▮▮▮

DOB (MM/DD/YYYY) If your qualifying person is age 19 or older in 2018, go to line 3a. If not, go to line 4 . . . . . 08/17/2015

a   Was your qualifying person a full time student under age 24 in 2018? . . . . **3a** [ ] Yes   [ ] No

b   Was your qualifying person permanently and totally disabled in 2018? . . . . **3b** [ ] Yes   [ ] No

4 Enter qualifying person's gross income in 2018. See instructions . . . . [   ]

5 Number of days your qualifying person lived with you during 2018. See instructions . . . . [   ]

When calculating the total number of days your qualifying person lived with you, you may include any days your qualifying person was temporarily absent from your home. For example, illness, education, business, vacation, military service, and incarceration. In the event of a birth or death of your qualifying person during the year, enter 365 days.

For Privacy Notice, get FTB 1131 ENG/SP.   098   8481184   FTB 3532 2018

ABOUT THE AUTHOR

Brian D. Lerner is an Immigration Lawyer and runs a National Immigration Law Firm for nearly 30 years. He is an attorney who is a certified specialist that might help in Immigration & Nationality Law as issued by the California State Bar, Board of Legal Specialization. Attorney Lerner is an expert in Immigration Law, Removal and Deportation, Citizenship, Waiver and Appeals.

He has been a licensed attorney since 1992 and started the Law Offices of Brian D. Lerner, APC. The immigration practice consists of Immigration and Nationality Law, and everything involved with and regarding immigration which includes citizenship, investment visas, family and employment visas, removal and deportation hearings, appeals, waivers, adjustment, consulate processing and all types of immigration and citizenship matters.

He has represented clients from all over the U.S. and in many countries around the world. One side of his practice is dedicated to keeping people in the U.S. and fighting for their immigration rights, while another side is to get people back who have been deported and removed from the U.S.

Also, there is the affirmative part of Immigration Law which Brian Lerner has helped numerous people come into the U.S. on business visas, investment visas, student visas, fiancée and marriage visas, religious visas and many more. Attorney Lerner has helped immigrants who are victims of crime and domestic violence or ones that are married to abusers.

In other words, Attorney Lerner has a firm that helps people all over the U.S. He has dedicated significant time to preparing numerous petitions and applications for you to get at a fraction of the price of hiring an attorney. He says it is the next best thing to a real attorney because they are real petitions prepared by an expert.

www.ingramcontent.com/pod-product-compliance
Lightning Source LLC
Chambersburg PA
CBHW051800200326
41597CB00025B/4628